THE PELICAN GUIDE TO
Hillsborough

THE PELICAN GUIDE TO

Hillsborough

Historic Orange County, North Carolina

Lucile Noell Dula

PELICAN PUBLISHING COMPANY

GRETNA 1989

First edition, 1979
Second edition, 1989

Library of Congress Cataloging-in-Publication Data

Dula, Lucile Noell.
  The Pelican guide to Hillsborough, historic Orange County, North
Carolina / Lucile Noell Dula.—2nd ed.
    p. cm.
  Half title: Hillsborough.
  Bibliography: p.
  Includes index.
  ISBN 0–88289–719–5
  1. Hillsborough (N.C.)—Description—Guide-books. 2. Historic
buildings—North Carolina—Hillsborough—Guide-books.
3. Hillsborough (N.C.)—Description—Tours. 4. Walking—North
Carolina—Hillsborough—Guide-books. I. Pelican Publishing
Company. II. Title. III. Title: Guide to Hillsborough, historic
Orange County, North Carolina. IV. Title: Hillsborough.
F264.H7D84 1989
917.56'565—dc19   88-34645
                                                              CIP

Manufactured in the United States of America

Published by Pelican Publishing Company, Inc.
1101 Monroe Street, Gretna, LA 70053

To my husband, Thomas,
and sons, Hunter and Harry,
whose support enabled me to complete this book,
and in memory of my late parents,
Frederick and Mary Lloyd Noell,
whose faith helped me to begin it.

"Town Crier" at the Town Hall (Mike Runkle)

Contents

Preface   9

Hillsborough, A Brief History   13

PART I: Tell-Tale Houses   19

PART II: A Walking Tour   53

Conclusion   109

Map   112

Key to Map   114

Appendix   117

Bibliography   119

Index   121

Mementoes (Frances Cox Taylor)

Preface

The historic town of Hillsborough is not an ordinary place. Here the old houses are private residences, and the noteworthy public buildings are used for community functions.

Hillsborough is also a place that must be seen stereoscopically if it is seen at all, for it is filled with facts, fantasy, and folklore—all as tangible as the orange-red clay which sometimes influences its stories. Throughout these tales—the real, the imaginary, and the semitrue—there are the characters that produce the action, and the sites and artifacts that have become parts of our lives. These include a small river, three molehills we call mountains, fourscore old houses and public buildings, an ancient tower clock, old gardens, specimen trees, and such small mementoes as a century-old figurine, a cowbell, and a Perfec Steriograph (patented 1903). All of these are parts of the Hillsborough story because they combine to produce the three-dimensional pictures which make the town unlike any other historic site in North Carolina.

Dickson House (Quentin Patterson)

THE PELICAN GUIDE TO
Hillsborough

Hillsborough, A Brief History

It is unique to discover a town in the United States which has evaded the hectic pace of twentieth-century living and preserved a major part of its past with a minimum of fanfare. Located about twelve miles from Durham and a thirty-eight-mile drive from the capital in Raleigh, Hillsborough is one of North Carolina's most historic and picturesque places. Platted by mapmaker-surveyor William Churton on a four-hundred-acre tract north of the Eno River, the county seat of Orange County has been making history since it was founded in 1754. Since the 1960s it has also been working harder to preserve what the past has left it.

At first the town was given a succession of names—Orange (like the county), Corbinton (or Corbin Town), Childsburg after two of the Earl of Granville's land agents, and in 1766, Hillsborough, after Wills Hill, the Earl of Hillsborough, who later served as secretary of state for the colonies. Then the name was shortened—no doubt to save time—first to Hillsboro' and eventually Hillsboro. However in 1965 the North Carolina General Assembly verified the fact that the spelling had never been officially changed, and as someone wrote, "The UGH was put back."

During its early years, a number of factors combined to earn Hillsborough the title "the capital of the Back Country." First, in 1767 Orange was the most populous county in the province, with an area so large that its northern boundary was the Virginia line. Since the major colonial roads crossed here, the town quickly became a trading center, and its prestigious position as a prominent county seat gave it political power as well.

William Churton Marker (Linda Kirby)

Court sessions brought many people to town, including judges and lawyers, and the county officials usually lived in the county seat. Sometimes these court officials were interested in personal gain. It is therefore understandable that the Regulator movement centered in Orange County. Organized in 1768 to oppose what they considered corrupt practices in local government administration, the organization collapsed after a two-hour battle at Alamance against Governor William Tryon and the militia on May 16, 1771. Six men, two whose names remain unknown, were hanged at a wooded spot outside the town limits on June 19, 1771. Alamance was not the first battle of the American Revolution, but it did focus attention on two serious problems: poor administration in local government and sectional domination by the East. In the Constitutional Convention of 1835, the cause of the Regulators would triumph.

Throughout the colonial period, Hillsborough was the center of other political activities. The Provincial Congress of 1775, re-enacted two hundred years later, convened here, as did the General Assemblies of 1778, 1780, 1782, 1783, and 1787. The British general, Charles Lord Cornwallis, also paid a visit in 1781, at which time he set up camp and invited "faithful and loyal subjects to repair, without loss of time with their arms and ten days provisions . . ." and was surprised when only a few responded. It was during this five-day visit that he had his men lay stones for 150 yards along King and Churton streets, paving which remained until 1909. Also, on February 22 he raised the Royal Standard in front of Orange County's second courthouse (the same site as the fourth, which is still standing). Ironically, the twenty-one-gun salute to King George III was fired on the forty-ninth birthday of the man who would defeat Cornwallis at Yorktown in October of that year and later become the first president of a new country—another George—Washington.

It was in Hillsborough, too, that the Constitutional Convention met in 1788 and voted against ratification of the Constitution. This was an important piece of legislation because it was this convention that recommended the Constitution contain a Bill of Rights.

Throughout its early history, Hillsborough attracted the educated, the energetic, and the imaginative, and together they helped shape the character of the town. It is no wonder then that these able individuals—many who came from other provinces—would provide North Carolina with eight superior court judges, two supreme court justices, and one man, William A. Graham, who was governor, United States senator, secretary of the navy, and a Whig candidate for vice-president.

Another factor benefitting Hillsborough was its equable climate, which attracted the well-to-do Easterners who found the long journey more endurable than the mosquitoes and malaria that were so prevalent near the marshlands. Many of them either bought or constructed houses. Moorefields, built by Alfred Moore in 1785, and the Hasell-Nash House by Eliza G. Hasell (ca. 1818–1819) are examples.

After the collapse of the Regulator movement, however, Hillsborough faced adverse circumstances. Guilford County was formed in 1770 from land taken from Orange and Rowan counties. A series of partitions after that reduced the vast area that had once belonged to Orange. Even after some substantial losses, the movement to make Hillsborough the state capital continued. However, in 1792 a Wake County site, now Raleigh, was chosen. The final blows came in 1849 when Alamance County was formed, and in 1881 with the creation of Durham County, for the major industries were located in these areas. Stripped of almost 90 percent of its territory, Orange was reduced to an area of approximately four hundred square miles, and Hillsborough was left mostly with memories of things past.

Today, however, there is a renewed interest in that past, for the people living in the small county seat have discovered that much of the heritage remains. Although many historic landmarks are gone, destroyed by fire, time, and sometimes by near-sighted citizens, much has been preserved. Today there are more than seventy-five eighteenth- and nineteenth-century buildings and a number of early twentieth-century structures in the Greater Hillsborough area. More than a dozen are listed in the National Register of Historic Places, and one is a National Historic Landmark. In August 1973 Historic Zoning was approved, and in October 1973 the Historic District was designated a National Historic District.

A survey of Hillsborough's early buildings reveals some unusual footnotes: there was a local brickyard in the mid-1700s, but the eighteenth-century houses are frame, and there are no remaining public buildings from that century. The oldest public building is the Presbyterian Church, completed in 1816.

Hillsborough's architecture also tells us much about its history. Beginning as a "mansion house" to meet William Churton's specifications, a "Habitable House of Stone Brick Squared Loggs Dovetailed or Frame and Shingled on the sd. Lott, not less than twenty feet in Length and sixteen feet in Breadth," many were enlarged to meet the needs of growing families. In general, "mansion houses" have lost their identity when minor alterations have been made, but are distinguishable when the changes are major, such as the addition of a second story or one or more wings. Some of the finer Hillsborough houses are examples of three types of architecture: Piedmont, the tall, narrow frame house with a long rear wing; the one-and-a-half-story Tidewater with narrow dormer windows; and the tripartite with its high central block and flanking wings.

The interiors of many landmarks also have distinctive features. Fine examples are the Chinese Chippendale stair railing at Moorefields, the woodwork and large-scale rooms at Ayr Mount, and the reeded mantels in a number of homes.

Three public landmarks in the National Register are the Old Courthouse, a Greek Revival structure designed and built by native architect-brick mason John Berry, the Masonic Hall, also Greek Revival, which he may have built, and St. Matthew's Episcopal Church, Gothic Revival, which he probably had a hand in. A number of other fine buildings also bear his mark in one way or another, including the Burwell School and Sans Souci, both in the National Register, the Peter Browne Ruffin house, and Sunnyside, Berry's suburban home. He also built the United Methodist Church and aided in building the First Baptist Church.

Today Hillsborough is aware of its heritage and is willing to share it. However, this is a unique town, for here the historic landmarks are all in use. Although Cornwallis would not find many of the buildings he saw in 1781, he would have no trouble locating old sites. The street names—Tryon, Queen, King, Churton, Hasell, Wake, Margaret Lane—are the same as they were before the American Revolution, and the street map adopted in 1766 is simple to follow. Available also is a town map drawn by Swiss surveyor Claude Joseph Sauthier. Completed in October 1768 for Governor William Tryon, it does not include names but is so exact that boundary lines and old wells can still be located.

There are other features, too, that distinguish Hillsborough from the average town. These include a variety of secondary buildings. There are separate kitchens, both frame and brick, meat houses, well houses, servants' quarters, necessaries, smokehouses, law offices, and milk houses, all left from the plantation era. The one- or two-story kitchens and the law offices have fireplaces, and many well houses have distinctive finials.

Hillsborough is also a place where everybody arrives with a

handful of plants and a pair of green thumbs. There are box-woods, vegetable and flower gardens, hardwoods, evergreens, and flowering trees that outnumber the people. The projects are both large—like the arboretum Paul Cameron planted on his estate in 1857—and small—like the garden where Maggie Tudor planted okra seeds saved each year from a fine variety her mother brought from the Sandhills in 1887. Perhaps that is why the roots of the people are deep and why "the little town Cornwallis would recognize" still strives to preserve the best of its past in spite of the phenomenal growth of the areas around it.

PART I
Tell-Tale Houses

Mayor's rack and robe in the Town Hall (Mike Runkle)

Introduction

Hillsborough, platted in 1754, has come full circle. Like its better known Virginia neighbor, Williamsburg, the town shone during the eighteenth century, languished during the nineteenth, and regained much of its lost splendor in the twentieth.

In most ways Hillsborough's early renown was achieved without benefit of industries or factories inside its corporate limits because—tradition says—the affluent landowners did not want to hear the whistles and would not sell their land. Still, the strategically located village, once called "the capital of the Back Country," somehow attracted people from far and wide, and some of the houses they built are historic residences now.

Until the 1960s, almost every old house was lived in by either descendants of the original owners or native families who had lived in them from 50 to 150 years. During that decade, however, people from far-flung places once more came to Hillsborough, bought and restored old landmarks, and became a part of Piedmont North Carolina's most historic town. This section includes only a handful of the stories about some of the homes and the people who have left their fingerprints on the houses, the community, or both.

WILLIAM COURTNEY'S YELLOW HOUSE

Although the Courtney House was once a tavern allegedly visited by Lord Cornwallis, it is best known as Hillsborough's first telephone office. In 1906 the Morris Telephone Company tried to rent a building here, but found it difficult; the townspeople were afraid the equipment might be struck by lightning. Finally, Henry Murdock agreed to rent them a room in his home (the Courtney House), and his daughter, Mamie, became the first switchboard operator.

When she began her duties, there were fifty patrons and she was paid fifteen dollars a month and given time off to attend church on Sundays. She liked to work and continued as "Central" after her marriage to William A. Gordon. When her husband died in 1920, she had three children to support, but by then there were more telephones in Hillsborough and her salary was larger. The two sons graduated from the University of North Carolina, and the daughter from Peace College.

"Miss Mamie" had only one serious illness while she was with the telephone company: appendicitis. She was in the hospital for thirty days, and the family manned the switchboard. Although she was seriously ill, she later said she never doubted she would recover, but almost everyone else was doubtful.

There are many stories about the ways "Central" served the people of Hillsborough (then spelled Hillsboro). For many years there was no public water system, and the local "bucket brigade" had to be alerted when there was a fire. There were also only a few officers, all of them with double duties, and they had to be summoned by Miss Mamie. Once when a number of people were seriously ill and several deaths occurred within a short time, she stayed at the switchboard for forty-two hours to provide emergency assistance and get messages to distant relatives.

Many World War II GI's learned, too, that Hillsborough's efficient telephone operator provided them with a lifeline home. Once she was up virtually all night when some local sailors arrived in California, forgot the time difference, and began to make calls after midnight Eastern Standard Time.

Miss Mamie left the switchboard in 1948 when Morris installed the dial system, but remained briefly to handle routine duties. When the townspeople presented her with a check—small by current standards—she said she had given less than she had received. However, Hillsborough's subscribers were grateful to an operator who rarely rang wrong numbers, made unlisted numbers unnecessary, and made prank/crank calls impossible.

Today the old telephone office bears the name of William Courtney, a prominent early Quaker. However, to those who remember the voice that said, "Number, please," the house will always be the office of Mamie Gordon, "Central" for forty-two years.

William Courtney's Yellow House (Quentin Patterson)

Patterson-Palmer House (Charles H. Cooper, *Herald-Sun Papers*)

PATTERSON-PALMER HOUSE

Margaret Lane is an old street, and the house on the corner reminds many of Williamsburg. Viewed through the eyes of childhood, however, it becomes once more an unpainted dwelling (later barn-red) with a long north porch, and the dormer windows, removed by a former owner, existing only in our dreams.

It is easy to recall, too, the creaking swing on the porch and the double-file walk that separated the ancient boxwoods. My grandmother, Emma Williams Lloyd, always wanted to replace the dormers, but my grandfather, Alex, whom I never knew, died in 1909 and there was only money for necessities. The kitchen was eventually moved from the basement, and finally lights, water, and a bathroom were added. When she died in 1952, however, many things still needed to be done to the old house.

In 1960 my aunt, Ida Lloyd, sold the property to Mrs. Helen Hill and restoration began. Later, Drs. Ronald and Mary Ann Witt also helped restore the house to almost its original condition. Today it is a colonial gray, the dormers have been restored, and the box-woods, now about two hundred years old, have converged in the middle of the walk. The long porch, too, has been replaced by a smaller one and a narrow porch added at the back.

Changes have also been made inside. The partitions which had created two extra bedrooms have been removed from the hall and living room, and these areas restored to their original proportions.

The fireplaces have been supplemented by a modern system, but we were never cold in the old days. We only shivered when the ghost in the dining room, somewhere near the hearth, started his nightly knocking.

The lateral hall, even then almost as large as most rooms, was another of our favorite spots. Except when the weather was very cold, it was an ideal place to stretch out on the carpeted floor and see 3-D pictures in an old Perfec Steriograph.

I also remember the small fireplace in the west room, unused for several years until it was rediscovered by Mrs. Helen Hill. One corner of the ceiling in this room was low, a fact we recalled after bumping our heads over and over again.

The basement was another place of mystery because some of the floors were dirt, and it was easy to pretend that we were exploring for buried treasure. We did not know then that a shoemaker had once had a shop there, or that one day somebody would discover a tremendous rock in the basement hall and find it difficult to move.

In the 1920s, transportation was difficult and there were no school buses. Therefore, a number of high school students came to Hillsborough and stayed in town during the school year. At various times my grandmother provided room and board for two nieces and an additional girl, but never more than two at a time. She also rented a room and served meals to two or three people who regularly attended court sessions. Somehow she was able to cook for eight or ten people when the occasion required, in spite of the fact that her kitchen was as small as most pantries.

Hillsborough native Elizabeth Matheson now owns the old homeplace, and the wide boards of the lateral hall floor are no longer hidden by a faded carpet. However, the redecorated rooms have retained the warmth of the old weather-beaten frame house, and through the 3-D lenses of childhood a slow-moving porch swing still invites children to spend a lazy afternoon.

TAMARIND

In 1950 Walter Carroll, then a staff writer for the *Durham Morning Herald*, wrote an article appropriately titled "The Strudwicks— Family of Artists." The Sunday feature told the story of wood-carver Shepperd Strudwick (1868–1961) and his three sons, portrait painters Clement (1900–1958) and Edmund (1909–1973), and actor Shepperd, Jr. (1907–1983). Today a story of the house the elder Strudwick built in 1903, christened Tamarind by the present owners, might be aptly titled, "The Kennedy House—a Masterwork of Art."

From the beginning, the house was destined to become an art masterpiece. First, ecclesiastical architect Ralph Adams Cram (1863–1942), a brother-in-law of Susan Read Strudwick (1875–1960), designed the house. The result is an excellent example of his admiration "for the conviction, structural truth, and attention to detail of medieval buildings." Although he was America's foremost Gothic architect, he designed Georgian-style buildings at Sweetbriar College, used a combination of Spanish-Moorish-Texan styles at Rice University, and was sufficiently interested in Japanese architecture to study it and help introduce the style to Americans. It was therefore a challenge to the New England-born Cram to master another style and design a Southern country home with Gothic touches for a North Carolina gentleman and his Virginia-born wife. The imposing frame structure on Churton Street, built on an acre lot just north of the former site of an earlier house (ca. 1833), is the result.

Although the blueprints were altered to make the eventual house more Southern, the classical and turn-of-the-century features that remain make the residence more unusual and artistic. For example, the visitor to Tamarind is aware of the six square wooden columns at the front, but may not notice that the two central ones are farther apart than the remaining four. Such spacing allows the columns to line up with the door and windows without making the hall extremely narrow or the flanking rooms unnecessarily wide.

The same precise attention to details is also evident in the roof design. In spite of its unusual structure, the standing-seam metal roof, with each seam separately welded, fits the house compactly and adds strength and unity to the lines of the exterior.

The interior is also a combination of many distinctive features. Here the house blends the formal and informal characteristics of an elegant but practical residence. The panelled hall, parlor, and library at the front provide the formal touches, and the back portion, with its adjoining courtyard, adds the living quarters required by a family.

Tamarind (John P. Kennedy, Jr.)

In the beginning the house was designed for a fireplace or stove in each room, but today there are seven fireplaces, each equipped with brass or wrought-iron andirons. Originally, too, there was a single bathroom, one of Hillsborough's earliest.

When Cram designed the high-ceilinged house, he planned to plaster the ceilings, but the senior Strudwick objected because one of his sisters had been struck by a piece of plaster. Perhaps, too, the woodcarver who fashioned crosses for the Presbyterian and Methodist churches, as well as stagecoaches and the Uncle Remus characters, preferred the warmer qualities of wood.

Throughout the house there are also many other interesting uses of wood which must have delighted him. There are pine floors in main rooms, oak in the more traveled areas, and all of the downstairs rooms except a bedroom and the butler's pantry are panelled up to the chair rail. The panelling, designed and installed with exceptional care, varies from dark-stained in the front hall to painted softwoods in other areas. All of the woodwork is custom-made, too, except around the doors and windows. To avoid what Strudwick considered an unnecessary expense, this trim is turn-of-the-century instead of classical. The leaded glass in the dining room is also of a later period, and some of the woodwork in the hall appears to be.

The Kennedys have made many improvements since they bought the house in 1972. They have already completed such prosaic tasks as repairing leaks, replacing floors and plaster, adding new heating and plumbing systems, and rewiring most of the house. They have also repainted and redecorated all of the dwelling and added chandeliers which range in style from antique to contemporary. All are crystal except the wooden Italian baroque fixture, a family heirloom, which hangs above the long banquet table in the dining room. One crystal chandelier is from Barbara Kennedy's mother's apartment in Hampton Court Palace, England and resembles those in the Phyfe Room at Winterthur. Before it could be shipped, it had to be dismantled, and upon arrival, reassembled and rewired.

Even in a town noted for its flowers, trees, and shrubs, the plants at Tamarind are unusual. The ancient beech at the front and an undisciplined wisteria vine which measures five feet in circumference are older than the present house. There are also an enormous crepe myrtle, huge pecans, and an ancient rose with a crown eighteen inches wide. Susan Read Strudwick loved her garden, where a circular brick sundial measured the hours in a more leisurely fashion than today's electronic devices. The Kennedys also love it, and they have cleared stumps, put steps in the walk to the old formal garden, and simplified it by combining a number of smaller flower beds into several larger ones. Broccoli and English peas have been planted in one bed, day lilies have replaced some rosebushes, and additional roses have been planted in the arbor. The original brick patterns in the formal garden were rediscovered, and railroad ties were used to support the terraces, "which taught me how the pyramids were built," Barbara Kennedy says.

Today a mammoth old magnolia towers above the south upstairs bedroom window, and in the boxwood garden a stone bench has been inscribed with a line from Poe's sonnet "To Science": ". . . the summer dream beneath the Tamarind tree." Since Shepperd Strudwick, Jr., played Edgar Allan Poe in the Hollywood movie of the poet's life, both the line and the name Tamarind are appropriate. As the summer days move slowly across the face of Susan Read Strudwick's sundial, it may not be difficult to imagine the appearance of Uncle Remus and his characters to reenact their stories for a sensitive woodcarver who was once the head of the household of a "family of artists."

UNITED METHODIST CHURCH

In 1903 the Reverend Samuel F. Nicks attended the Methodist Conference in Goldsboro, North Carolina to receive his first appointment as a minister, and on November 7, 1945, he went back to the same city to retire. It was particularly fitting to those who live in the Durham Methodist District that he should have completed the circle at the place where he received his first assignment and that he should remain in Hillsborough (spelled Hillsboro then), the center of the district. There was another record that he set also: he served forty-two years in the district in which he was born.

United Methodist Church (Kevin Meredith, *News of Orange County*)

Beginning his work of serving seven churches at an annual salary of $470, Mr. Nicks had no method of traveling except by horse and buggy. One church was eighteen miles from the parsonage, and he traveled at times when his lap robe was veneered with a thin coating of ice and the buggy wheels were solid circles of frozen mud. He was often the first person to arrive at church, and many Sundays he began his day's work by building a fire. On his first charge Mr. Nicks began his work of painting, repairing, and building new churches. By actually surveying the membership of his five country churches, he was soon able to get donations of timber for the building of a new church. The only materials that had to be purchased were doors, windows, shingles, and hardware. Timber was secured from the land of some church members, and it was made into lumber at a nearby sawmill.

In 1923 Samuel and Emma Woods Nicks and their six children moved to Hillsboro, the county seat of Orange County. While here, Mr. Nicks was called on to help settle a legal battle. He persuaded the opposing forces to settle their difficulties at home, and the solicitor—who remarked that this was a new experience for him— heartily approved.

In his building programs Mr. Nicks was substantially aided by the Duke foundation, which appropriated money to help construct churches. One was built with stone from the same quarries as the buildings on Duke University's West Campus.

After he served many other Methodist churches in the Durham Methodist District, Mr. Nicks and his wife returned to Hillsboro in 1940 for his final appointment. During his forty-two years in the Durham District he had been responsible for the construction of seven churches, sixteen others had been painted and repaired, and seven parsonages had been remodeled. When he retired in 1945, he bought the Faucette Place—the historic Ashe House—across the street from the Methodist parsonage. He died in 1946.

BURWELL SCHOOL

Dr. J. S. Spurgeon bought the house on the corner of Churton and Union streets from Charles M. Parks in 1894. For twenty years (1837–1857) it had housed the Burwell School, one of North Carolina's schools for young ladies. It was to be the Spurgeon's home for seventy-one years.

Many changes had been made in the house since the Burwells had closed their school. In the late 1800s, the Charles M. Parks family had hired Jule Kerner (originally Korner or Koerner) to remodel the house. He added gingerbread brackets to the exterior, removed two of the original mantels, and lowered the downstairs windows. These renovations were removed in the late 1960s, but this was after the Spurgeons had sold their old homeplace to the Historic Hillsborough Commission.

When the family moved to Hillsborough there were two girls. Later the spacious yard became a playground for six children—five girls and a boy. Their friends were attracted to the area because the lawn was particularly suitable for sledding and games. The older Spurgeons enjoyed sports and during the early years rode bicycles and skated on the Eno River. For many years the old campus also resembled a small farm, with a garden, a horse, a cow, pigs, and chickens.

Dr. Spurgeon practiced dentistry for sixty-two years.

In 1965 the Historic Hillsborough Commission bought the house the Spurgeon family had lived in since 1894—the only house the

Burwell School (Lucy Martin)

family ever had. The structure has been restored and is once again called the Burwell School. An old-fashioned garden where the Spurgeon children collected wild flowers has been restored by the Hillsborough Garden Club and appropriately dedicated to Carrie Waitt Spurgeon.

HILLSBOROUGH MILITARY ACADEMY

In 1858 Hillsborough was selected as the site of an outstanding military academy, known locally as the Barracks. The town was chosen because of its location on the North Carolina Railroad, which made it accessible, and its healthful climate. Until the completion of the buildings in 1860, the school operated in the Hillsborough Academy, with the first session opening on January 12, 1859.

Colonel Charles C. Tew, commandant, graduated from the Citadel with highest honors. The Hillsborough Military Academy, located about a mile and a half west of Hillsborough, was immediately successful. Modeling the school after the best military academies, Tew maintained high standards by stern discipline and competent instruction in such diverse areas as the exact sciences and modern languages.

When the cadets appeared in parades, they invariably received acclaim from those who saw them drill. One such occasion was the North Carolina State Fair in Raleigh, October 1860. A letter written to the editor of the Raleigh *Standard* (later reprinted in the *Hillsborough Recorder*, October 24, 1860) concerning their appearance stated: "The arrival of the Hillsborough Cadets on the Fairgrounds at Raleigh on Thursday last caused quite a sensation among citizens of your village. . . . It was indeed a handsome spectacle as the young soldiers, with cheeks flushed with vigorous health and sparkling with martial enthusiasm, filed, with 'proud and manly tread,' into the broad circle."

After the Ordinance of Secession was passed on May 20, 1861, Tew offered his services to his adopted state and was named colonel of the Second Regiment. He was killed in action at Sharpsburg on September 17, 1862. Major William Gordon, an assistant at the academy, served as supervisor after Tew left the school, but both failed. It closed in 1868.

Although the Hillsborough Military Academy is gone, the Commandant's House survives. It has been restored and is the home of Mr. and Mrs. Lucius Cheshire, Sr.

COLONIAL INN

No town can be as old as Hillsborough without producing both legends and oft-told tales. One story concerns Calvin and Octavia Strowd, innkeepers at the time of the Civil War. While Calvin was away with the Confederate army, news came that General Sherman's army was pursuing the army of General Joseph E. Johnston, and that they were headed for North Carolina. The route the Union general took would be determined by the roads the fleeing Johnston chose to travel. After they engaged in battle at Bentonville, Johnston retreated to Raleigh, and shortly afterward his army was seen traveling along the railroad tracks in the direction of Greensboro. The Hillsborough people knew this meant Sherman's army was not far behind. Octavia knew the Yankees would stop at the inn, so she had the loyal slaves drive the horses off in the direction of Durham, hoping that some friends would pick them up.

When the Yankees arrived, they lost no time in ransacking the inn. Going upstairs after the search, Mrs. Strowd found garments scattered over the floor in one of the rooms. Among the clothing were papers and her husband's Masonic apron. Seeing the latter, she decided to hang the apron from a stick and wave it from the window. When she saw a Union officer start forward, she went downstairs to meet him. The officer, a Mason, ordered the men to return all the property they had taken, to discontinue their search, and to leave the inn unmolested for the rest of their stay. From then until their departure the property was faithfully guarded, and even after Johnston surrendered at the nearby Bennett Place, the inn was unharmed.

Colonial Inn

HEARTSEASE

Dennis Heartt, a newspaper editor in Hillsborough for forty-nine years, was not a native North Carolinian. His father, an English sea captain, settled in New England, and Dennis was born in New Bedford, Connecticut, on November 6, 1783. Not much is known of his early years. In 1798 he moved to New Haven and became a printer to Read and Morse, the latter a brother of Samuel F. B. Morse, inventor of the telegraph. Although he was only fifteen, he was soon able to set up five thousand ems in half a day.

Heartsease (Mark Gordon)

While he was working in New Haven, he had an unusual experience. In setting type for Noah Webster he discovered an *i* had been omitted from *fashion* and he inserted it. The famous lexicographer proofread the copy, wrote *fashon* again, and the printer complied. However, Webster caught his error in the final proof and included the *i*. From then on, Heartt used this incident as an example of the irritations that occur almost exclusively in the field of journalism.

Dennis Heartt succeeded in his journalistic venture. His subscription list rose rapidly, and the *Recorder* soon exerted an influence far greater than its size. For a brief while he was joined by his son, Edwin, a talented journalist. However, the son died in 1855 only a few months after assuming his duties. In 1869 Heartt sold the paper to C. N. B. Evans & Son (of Milton), who sold it in 1871. When he became editor, Evans wrote, "We are conducting one of the oldest papers in the South—certainly the oldest in the State, and we desire its permanency. We make no appeals to our people, believing that if we prove worthy of our position, they will come to our support. . . ."

In assuming that the *Recorder* was North Carolina's first paper, the new editor was wrong, but few had such a long and happy existence. Even now it is possible to follow the happenings of that era and be influenced by them because so many copies of Dennis Heartt's paper have been preserved. This is especially gratifying in Hillsborough, for many who live here now are descendants of those who were making the news in the old *Recorder* from 1820 through 1869.

OLD TOWN CEMETERY

Impressive figures and great events lend historic significance to the old buildings and landmarks that abound in Hillsborough. However, the preservation of these sites requires the continued support of such organizations as the Hillsborough Historical Society, Inc., organized and chartered in 1962.

While the Historic Hillsborough Commission is engaged in such long-range projects as the restoration of the Burwell School, the Society generally concerns itself with beautifying historic spots by planting bulbs, shrubs, and trees, designating old homes and public buildings by brass plaques or wooden markers, and replacing old railings with wrought iron. Other activities have included extensive work in the Old Town Cemetery.

The first project, repairing the cemetery wall, was financed by the proceeds from a chicken barbeque supper. Other funds have been raised through sponsoring tours and conducting membership drives.

The restoration of gravesites has also been a major project of the Society. At the Old Town Cemetery some tombstones have been cleaned, repaired, and reset, and the stone wall around the burial ground and the brick wall around the Hooper lot have been restored.

An interesting discovery was made when workers uncovered a stone walk leading from a gate on Churton Street to the burial ground. A marble stone revealed, too, that during a time when transportation was difficult a young girl from Marlboro County,

South Carolina was buried here. Frances Elizabeth Coit, 15, died on June 4, 1852, while attending a boarding school here.

The epitaph for another young woman, Mary Holmes, 24, reads:

> She needs no formal record of her virtues on this cold marble. They are deeply graven on the tablets of many warm and loving hearts.

Here surrounded by box, dogwoods, and hundreds of daffodils, their resting places, like those about them, are kept beautiful by people concerned with the restoration and preservation of such historic sites. The Hillsborough Historical Society, Inc., is working to make Hillsborough's past a part of its present and future.

PETER BROWNE RUFFIN HOUSE (RUFFIN-SNIPES)

Hillsborough has a number of dwellings where ghosts are said to reside, but only the Peter Browne Ruffin House has a haunted room. It all started when an Alamance County man was hanged from an alcove for stealing a Bible. The owner promptly sold the room (most likely a one-room house) and carted it to Hillsborough, along with the ghost of the murdered man.

Since that time a number of things have happened which indicate his ghost dwells in the dining room. For instance, it has the only undependable fireplace in the house: it does not burn, it smokes. Then during the 1920s a carpenter working just above this area is said to have fallen and broken his leg. A ghost definitely had to be involved in the third accident. A number of years ago the present owners, Jack and Betty Snipes, decided to paint the interior of the house. They selected the colors, labeled each with the name of the room where it was to be used, and stored the sealed cans in the dining room. However, after the painters had worked awhile they discovered that the colors were wrong. An investigation revealed that somebody, or something, had switched the lids, and every can of paint was mislabeled. The error was corrected, but the dining room of the Peter Browne Ruffin House still bears the label "haunted."

Peter Browne Ruffin House (Ruffin-Snipes) (Linda Kirby)

ROULHAC-HAMILTON HOUSE

The Roulhac-Hamilton House has "the finest boxwoods in the area," and cypress trees the Reverend Moses Ashley Curtis is believed to have planted from seeds. However, there was a time when it was an unpainted, unoccupied frame dwelling better known for its ghosts. During those years the box and the trees made the setting more eerie, and anyone who passed it almost expected to see one "hant," in particular: a ghost someone had named Nancy Hamilton. Before dark, however, a group would occasionally venture across the street to the old house and knock on the front door.

Roulhac-Hamilton House (Kevin Meredith, *News of Orange County*)

It was late one afternoon when several teenagers decided to dart between the boxwoods and visit Nancy. They moved cautiously across the front porch, rapped several times, and waited for the expected echoes. This time, though, they were surprised to hear heavy footsteps, and they were too frightened to move. Suddenly the door opened and they faced a woman much too large to be their favorite ghost. They were halfway to the street when they realized the "intruder" was not Nancy Hamilton, but the owner of the house, Miss Lily Hamilton. They never learned why she had made an unexpected visit to the house that had been closed for so long, but this was the last reported visit anyone made to the Roulhac-Hamilton House until it was renovated by a later owner.

A REGULATOR STORY

There are many interesting stories about the Regulators who fought and lost the Battle of Alamance. One incident concerns a condemned man and his son's encounter with Governor William

Tryon. When Captain Messer was sentenced to hang, the boy asked the governor to hang him instead. Astonished, Tryon stormed: "Who told you to say that?" "No one," young Messer answered, "but if you hang my father, my mother will die and the children will perish." Momentarily touched, Tryon allegedly assured the boy that his father would not die that day. However, the governor's change of heart was short-lived, for Messer and five other Regulators were hanged on June 19, 1771.

The Regulator Marker (Mary R. Cole)

DICKSON HOUSE*

The Dickson House is a little gem of a mid-eighteenth-century farmhouse. Its fine woodwork and brickwork have survived 230 years or so with relatively little damage. No doubt this house saw much interesting history before and during the Revolution, but it was in the Civil War that the house came into special prominence. In the last days of that war the Dickson farm was headquarters for Confederate general Wade Hampton. His tattered, hungry troops camped in the fields around the house, and tradition says the general used the outbuilding, called "the office," as his own office.

When President Jefferson Davis gave consent to his ranking officer, General Joseph Johnston, to approach General Sherman concerning a possible surrender, General Johnston went to General Hampton's headquarters and from there, on April 17, 1865, set out by horseback to meet with General Sherman at Bennett Place, a farmhouse near Durham Station. The talks at Bennett Place were at first unsuccessful. General Johnston summoned to advise him two other Confederate leaders, General J. C. Breckenridge and Postmaster General John H. Reagan, and the three met early in the morning of April 18 in "the office." Later that day General Johnston returned to Bennett Place to meet with General Sherman, and this time the talks were successful. Although Washington ultimately rejected the liberal terms granted to the South, the surrender of April 18 effectively ended Confederate resistance in the middle South.

The Dickson Place has sometimes been called "the last headquarters of the Confederacy." This is an appropriate title in the sense that it was the last headquarters of the commander of the largest of the armies to surrender to Union forces, larger even than the army that Lee surrendered at Appomattox. It is doubtful that any other residence now standing in Piedmont North Carolina is as significant in Civil War history as the Dickson House.

The Dickson House and office originally stood at the southwest intersection of Interstate 85 and Highway 86, 1 1/4 miles from their present location in the center of Hillsborough. To save them from destruction, the Preservation Fund of Hillsborough purchased them in 1982 and moved them to a large lot in the center of town given by Mrs. Charles H. Blake in honor of her late husband, a noted historian of the town and county. Generous help was received from the Z. Smith Reynolds Foundation and the Mary Duke Biddle Foundation.

In 1983, the General Assembly, in response to a bill introduced by Rep. Anne Barnes, appropriated $35,000 to be used toward the restoration of the house. This sum has been carefully used under the supervision of the Division of Archives and History, and now the house is once more structurally sound.

The completion of the restoration, adhering to the high standard needed for a visitors' center, is estimated to cost $140,000. This sum will restore the interior, restore the office, rebuild two chimneys, put shingle roofs on the two buildings, install utilities, reimburse the Preservation Fund for money lent to the project, etc. It is hoped that the money can be raised by a combination of foundation grants and gifts from businesses and individuals.

The Dickson House, with its office, is the ideal place for a visitors' center. It is easily accessible to the interstate. There is ample on-street parking. The house is surrounded by interesting walking tours of historic sites, and it is a good place from which to arrange driving tours of all parts of the county.

One room of the house is large enough to accommodate a classroom of children or a busload of adults for a slide presentation or a lecture. Other rooms are suitable for exhibits. The buildings themselves illustrate many architectural principles significant to this region, and as we have pointed out, the house is a particularly good place from which to discuss Civil War history. With a little imagination, one can see General Joseph Johnston and General Wade Hampton talking under the big maple that used to stand by the office. Or one can imagine the hungry Confederate troops, as they were in the last days of the war, foraging over the farm in search of wild onions to be cooked as a vegetable.

Reprinted by permission of the Preservation Fund of Hillsborough, John P. Kennedy, Jr.

Highlands (Quentin Patterson)

HIGHLANDS

In the fall of the year 1844, on the site which is now Highlands, two rooms were built for use as a classical school by Mr. James H. Norwood and were used as such until January 1846 when Mr. Norwood moved to Asheville. The property was bought at that time by his brother-in-law, Mr. Andrew Mickle, and two rooms and a porch were added and the house used as a residence.

In 1849, Mr. Mickle moved to Chapel Hill, and the house was closed and remained vacant for some time before it was sold to Mr. E. D. McNair of Tarboro, North Carolina, who lived there for many years before returning in the late fifties to his old home. The property was then purchased by Mr. Paul C. Cameron and was rented to various people, including Mrs. Bettie Thompson, who was a refugee from Edenton, North Carolina and a sister of General G. B. Anderson. When General Joseph E. Johnston made a formal surrender to General Sherman at Bennett Place between Hillsborough and Durham, it was agreed that General Robert H. Anderson's Brigade of cavalry should remain for some days for the protection of the populace from stragglers. General Anderson's headquarters was in Mr. James Webb's lot, across from Mr. Cameron's property.

On the morning of May 4, 1865, when Federal officers were to receive the paroles of the Brigade, a severe wind made paper work out of doors impossible and permission was obtained from Mr. Cameron to use his house, vacant at that time. In the dining room, almost the last of the Confederate soldiers to surrender gave their paroles.

During the year 1877, Mr. Cameron added the rooms which comprise the present house and gave this property to his daughter, Annie Cameron Collins, for her lifetime, then to his grandson and namesake, Paul Cameron Collins, who lived there the remainder of his life, leaving it to his daughter and present owner, Elizabeth Collins. Highlands is located on Highway 70-A East.

OVER THE RIVER

Over the River was built about 1820 by Judge William Norwood and his wife Robina Hogg Norwood on an approximately twenty-acre tract adjoining the Eno River. It had been acquired from her father, James Hogg, and was located northwest from and adjoining his home, Poplar Hill. It originally consisted of two rooms down-stairs and two upstairs, with a small third room above a portion of the hall which intersected the house from front to back, and from which stairs afforded access from the cellar to the attic. It fronted the river and in its exterior appearance it was almost a mirror image of its parent home, Poplar Hill, with a shed roof porch across the south and chimneys on each end. The dining room was originally in the basement, with windows to the north and south and a fireplace on the east. Cooking was, of course, done in the outdoor kitchen.

James Webb, Jr., son of Dr. James Webb and his wife, Annie Alves Huske Webb, and the great-grandson of James Hogg,

Over the River (Thomas C. Wagstaff)

bought the property from the Norwoods in 1848, and it was he and his wife, Sarah Frances Cheshire Webb, who added the eastern wing to the house. The small one-story wing on the southeast corner, which dates from the original structure, was moved from the yard and connected to the house by H. Winder Webb early in this century. It was converted to use as an indoor kitchen about 1940 by James Webb Cheshire, whose mother, Annie Webb, was born at Over the River. She had made her home there until her marriage to her first cousin, Joseph Blount Cheshire, Jr. Upon the death of James Webb Cheshire, it was acquired by his oldest grandchild and wife, the current owners. It is the only historic home in Hillsborough which remains in the family of its original owner.

The old kitchen with its three fireplaces still stands, and Kansas, the original guesthouse, today serves as a playhouse. The original barn has been replaced by a much smaller one, and a reconstructed smokehouse is used for storage; the well house protects the old well and provides shelter to wasps, and the old ice pit is better known now as the snake pit.

MONTROSE

Hillsborough is a historic town (1754) where many eighteenth- and nineteenth-century houses have names and—like those of the characters in a Dickens novel—the names often reveal something about persons or places. Some, like "Nash-Hooper" and "Turner-Strudwick," simply designate people associated with the dwellings, while others, like "Maple Hill," "Moorefields," and "Chatwood," identify nature-lovers. "Sunnyside" faces east and "Sans Souci" (without care) and "Hardscrabble" (now a part of Durham County) signify the differences between the town mansion and the simpler country house of the same builder.

Other houses, however, are less easy to classify because so much depends on pronunciation. Decades ago, for example, I read the word *Montrose* (Mon-trose), called it "Mont-rose," and immediately associated it with the flower. Time has proven, however, that it would not have been a misnomer, for roses—the old-fashioned varieties noted for fragrance as well as beauty—have long flourished there, along with many other plants the owners have propagated to give pleasure or to preserve species.

The preamble to the Montrose story, however, began in 1781 when the tract was part of a larger estate, and the site of Lord Cornwallis's first encampment. It was that winter that the British general discovered that Hillsborough was not the sleepy little town it appeared to be, and that no red carpets would be rolled out for the Redcoats here. Sixty-one years later, William A. Graham (who would serve as governor of North Carolina, United States senator, and secretary of the Navy) bought a near-sixty-acre tract from that site, then owned by the Kirkland family. Graham named it "Montrose" for his Scottish ancestor, James Graham, Earl of Montrose, and built the first house, along with some outbuildings, on the property.

Although that house and a second one—also built by William Graham—were destroyed by fire, the outbuildings survived. One, his law office, was reputedly expanded and used as a family residence during the construction of the second dwelling. The present house—the third on the site—is a white frame mansion built by Graham's son, Major John Graham, in 1898 and remodeled by the governor's grandson, former lieutenant governor Alexander H. ("Sandy") Graham, Sr., and Kathleen Long Graham in 1948.

Craufurd and Nancy Goodwin bought Montrose from A. H. ("Sandy") Graham, Jr., and John Graham in 1977. It was fortunate that these people and this place found each other. Since 1963 the Goodwins had owned a house in Durham, with ample space for a garden, but that summer they visited England and Nancy discovered wild cyclamen. Later, she learned that it was an endangered species, and, by 1977, her avocation had become a crusade.

Since 1852, when the Grahams had returned from Washington following William's duties as secretary of the Navy, Montrose had always attracted people with "green fingers." In 1977, there were ancient trees on the site, a Tree Box that originated from a cutting taken from William Graham's grave, and a rock garden he had started while he was secretary of the Navy. His descendants had added many plants, including dwarf boxwoods, gladioli, jonquils, roses, and a scuppernong arbor, and had planted acres of vegetables and strawberries annually. With its meadows, woodlands, farmland, pond, and spacious dwelling, Montrose was the perfect place for Craufurd, a professor of economics at Duke University, to raise vegetables—particularly tomatoes—and for Nancy to grow miniature perennials—particularly cyclamen—from seed.

Because of the greed of retailers, who illegally collected the tubers from their natural habitat, and the unrest in the Third World, wild cyclamen was doubly endangered. Aware of the need for more seed-grown plants, Nancy Goodwin accelerated her program of propagation by germinating seeds indoors anywhere she could find the space: the basement, the windowsills, the piano studio. She also purchased additional seeds from reputable retailers. Originally, she raised the potted plants in a screened porch until her first greenhouse was completed in 1984.

Today, Montrose Nursery has two greenhouses and a gardener to help operate the business. Although Nancy does not advertise, there are 2,000 names on her mailing list and articles or items about the nursery have appeared in *American Horticulturist*, the *New York Times, Southern Living*, the *Daniel Morgan Register*, and the *News of Orange County*. These, along with the Montrose Nursery Catalog, have been more beneficial than paid-for promotions.

In the meantime, Nancy Goodwin grows eighteen of the twenty known species of cyclamen, tries to improve her plants, and crusades against the grubby-fingered merchants who strip the endangered plants from their native habitat and illegally distribute them to greedy buyers wherever they find them. By propagating seed-grown cyclamen, Montrose and a handful of other nurseries make legal plants available and increase the chance that each of these plants may produce 100 blossoms, from white to magenta, and live its allotted 100 years.

The house, which faces a busy street and whose next-door neighbor is an elementary school, seems to have also escaped the hubbub of the twentieth century and remains the headquarters of a horticultural Shangri-la.

Montrose (Thomas C. Wagstaff)

Moorefields (Thomas C. Wagstaff)

MOOREFIELDS*

As one of three host sites of the roving North Carolina General Assembly, eighteenth-century Hillsborough attracted many influential men, among them Wilmington's Alfred Moore, a Revolutionary War captain and one of North Carolina's foremost jurists.

In 1785 Moore built a summer home on 1,202 acres near the Eno River and Seven Mile Creek, and named it Moorefields. Orange County held its first Court of Common Pleas and Quarters on the site in 1752, two years before Hillsborough was founded.

Moore was then state attorney general. Later he became chief justice of the North Carolina Supreme Court, barely missed election to the U.S. Senate, and helped found the University of North Carolina at Chapel Hill. Moore's career of public service was capped in 1798, when he became the second North Carolinian appointed to serve as an associate justice on the U.S. Supreme Court.

The man for whom Moore County is named retired from the bench in 1805 and died five years later. Over the years most of Moorefields' land was sold off, but the house and surrounding acreage remained in the family until 1911. (A stone-walled family graveyard remains under a vine-shrouded tulip poplar several hundred yards southwest of the house.)

In 1949 the property was purchased by UNC French professor Edward Thayer Draper-Savage, later discovered to be related by marriage to the Moores. Draper-Savage restored the house, which won designation to the National Register of Historic Places on April 25, 1972. A sculptor, he also designed lawns, flower beds, a formal hedge garden, and park.

Upon Draper-Savage's death in 1978, a nonprofit "Effie Draper Savage—Nellie Draper Dick Memorial Foundation for the Preservation of 'Moorefields'" took charge of the property. (Draper-Savage is buried just west of the house, among his beloved cats.) The Moorefields Foundation is administered by the Trust Department of Central Carolina Bank, which oversaw stabilization and renovation of the house in 1983.

The house at Moorefields is architecturally distinguished as one of the earliest examples of the Federal style in North Carolina. The exterior appears very much as it must have in 1785.

The building features a spacious "Great Hall," with a well-executed reeded mantel and furniture and family portraits left by Draper-Savage. A rare Chinese Chippendale staircase marks the tall central hallway, and the house's matching two-room wings feature additional furniture and artwork, as well as space for meetings and displays. Alfred Moore carefully situated his house atop a hill astride the prevailing summer breeze. According to legend, the Moores enjoyed the house's cooling charms from May through the third hard frost in October. Today a curator inhabits Moorefields year round.

Fifty oaks planted around the house in 1785 combined with the overhanging front porch to cool further the interior. Most of those trees have died, but red oaks were recently planted to take their place. A quarter-mile of hedges, four acres of lawns and wild flowers, flower beds, wooded camping sites, nature trails, and forty acres of permanent pasture further grace Moorefields. The grounds are maintained as a wildlife refuge, and every effort is made to work in consonance with nature.

The Moorefields Foundation is devoted to preserving the house and grounds at Moorefields, and to making those resources accessible to the public. The property is available for camping, use by artists, and as the site for small group conferences and receptions. Moorefields is open by appointment only, and modest contributions are required to facilitate use.

Story by Barry Jacobs, Caretaker.

PART II
A Walking Tour

The Commandant's House (Thomas C. Wagstaff)

Introduction

Although Hillsborough's historic houses are private residences not generally open to the public, some can be seen during the biennial tours in April of the odd-numbered years. It is also possible to visit one or two homes at other times by making prior arrangements with the Hillsborough Historical Society, Inc., Box 871, Hillsborough, North Carolina 27278. Although some of the houses are outside the corporate limits, many can be viewed on foot, and the others are easily accessible by car.

The Pelican Guide to Hillsborough, North Carolina contains some of the places cited in the "Historic Hillsborough" brochure (1986), published by the Society, and others that have been open on tours or listed in some of the Walking Tour guides. The map and key have been provided through their courtesy and reprinted by permission.

OLD ORANGE COUNTY COURTHOUSE

The heart of Hillsborough's Historic District is the Fourth Orange County Courthouse. Constructed at a cost of $10,000 ($2,000 more than the terms of the builder's contract), it is native architect-builder John Berry's masterpiece. When it was dedicated in 1844, newspaper editor Dennis Heartt declared, "It is not surpassed by any courthouse in the state; and . . . it is perhaps not surpassed in the Union." His judgment was substantiated in 1963 when the structure was designated a Historic American Building.

Old Orange County Courthouse (Quentin Patterson)

The handsome red brick Greek Revival building has a Doric portico and the original hand-forged window panes. Designed to house the county offices on the main floor and the courtroom upstairs, it remained in use even though the fifth courthouse was officially opened in 1954. The Orange County Board of Education used the first floor until the Administration Building was completed in 1973, and the Orange County Historical Museum occupied the second floor until 1983.

In designing the building, Berry studied Asher Benjamin's pattern books and took some interior details, including stair brackets, from Benjamin. It is believed that the entrance hall was originally two stories, with a double stairway opposite the front door. Some remodeling was done during the 1880s but the changes were not drastic.

Renovations were made during the 1980s when the Orange County Commissioners realized the need for additional court space. The exterior was cleaned and repaired, and the white columns and other woodwork painted. Some shrubs and bushes, including the hedge that surrounded the building, were removed, making the red bricks, the columns, and the clock more dominant.

Inside work included renovating the offices and the courtroom and purchasing a new judge's bench and a jury box. A modern heating and cooling system, new stairwells, and an elevator have made the building more comfortable and accessible without changing its basic structure.

Oil portraits of Chief Justice Thomas Ruffin and Governor William Graham, given by preservationist-financier Richard H. Jenrette, hang in the courtroom. They were presented to Orange County in a ceremony held in the Old Courthouse on April 16, 1987.

Southeast corner of East King and Churton streets.

TOWN CLOCK AND CUPOLA

The cupola of the Old Courthouse, home of the Town Clock, has three floors. The first houses the two 500-pound weights that swing the pendulum and strike the bell; the second contains the parts of the mechanism, and the third the two belfry bells. The clock is of uncertain origin, but tradition claims it was given to the town by a representative of King George III. Dr. Frank P. Albright of Old Salem, who has made a study of eighteenth-century clocks, wrote me, "There is a tradition, possibly it is more than a tradition, that the Hillsborough clock was made in England and sent to Hillsborough in 1769. The workmanship of the clock and the history as far as known beyond tradition, seem to indicate that the clock was made in England."

Since 1846 the clock has been in its present location. Originally it was probably placed in the tower of the old St. Matthew's Church, which burned in 1793, and later in the Market House tower.

Southeast corner of East King and Churton streets.

THE BURKE MARKER

South Churton Street, just west of the Old Courthouse.

Burke Marker (Lucy Martin)

Norwood-Jones Law Office (Linda Kirby)

THE WILLIAM CHURTON MARKER

106 East Margaret Lane.

NORWOOD-JONES LAW OFFICE

This one-story brick office (ca. 1800) was probably built by William Norwood (1766–1842), who practiced law in Hillsborough and served as superior court judge from 1820 to 1836. It was later used by Cadwallader Jones and by John Wall Norwood, a member of the General Assembly (1858), state senator (1872), and a longtime advocate of scientific farming. This building, formerly the Veterans Service Office, is presently used by the Orange County Commission for Women.

131 Court Street.

WILLIAM COURTNEY'S YELLOW HOUSE

The William Courtney House, once known as the Yellow House, is one of Hillsborough's oldest and most interesting structures. Probably built around 1768, it was the home of William Courtney, a Quaker. During its early years it was a tavern and from 1906 through 1948 served as the local office of the Morris Telephone Company. It was here, too, that the Methodist leader, Bishop Francis Asbury, held services in 1780, and Charles Lord Cornwallis spent some time in 1781.

The interior of the house is noted for its fine panelling and moldings. The brick office which stood east of the house is gone, but the unusual square well house remains.

141 East King Street.

DICKSON HOUSE

The Dickson House, a two-story dwelling, was built in the eighteenth century and renovated during the 1930s. In 1983 it was moved from Highway 86 South, adjacent to the post office, and is being restored as a visitors' center.

Southeast corner of East King and Cameron streets.

SEVEN HEARTHS

Seven Hearths, a house built on five levels, is an excellent example of Piedmont architecture. The central block which was the original house was probably built earlier than 1800. Barnaby Cabe may have been the builder.

Interesting features include its huge chimneys, reeded mantels, and seven fireplaces. Africa Parker, a freedman, once operated a stillhouse located near the western boundary of the lot. The property is sometimes referred to as the "Stillhouse Lott," and the stream is called "the Stillhouse branch." A large specimen magnolia now stands near the site of the stillhouse.

157 East King Street.

Seven Hearths (Elisabeth Stagg)

THE REGULATOR MARKER

A bronze marker inside a wrought-iron fence commemorates the spot where six Regulators were hanged by order of a Tory court on June 19, 1771. Since two of the men were not named, they are referred to as our "first unknown soldiers."

The exact site of the common unmarked grave is not known, but it is believed to be nearer the Eno River. The marker, however, has been placed east of the Orange County Board of Education building and south of St. Matthew's Episcopal Church.

St. Mary's Road.

ST. MATTHEW'S EPISCOPAL CHURCH

The present St. Matthew's Church was built in 1825, following the reorganization of St. Matthew's Parish the year before. The original building, a Church of England, was built prior to 1768 and burned ca. 1793. Following the American Revolution no established church existed, and the first St. Matthew's was used by other denominations, ultimately the Presbyterians. When plans were made to reorganize the parish in 1824, Thomas Ruffin gave the land because it was where Anne Kirkland had accepted his proposal of marriage.

St. Matthew's is a beautiful Gothic Revival building, probably designed by Francis Lister Hawks, grandson of John Hawks, architect for Tryon's Palace in New Bern. John Berry is believed to have assisted in building the church.

Throughout the years there have been many alterations: the tower was added in 1830 and the gallery in 1835; the tower rebuilt in 1850; exposed-beam roof, triplet window, and recessed window installed in 1868; and the spire added and the wainscoting replaced in 1868 or 1875.

There are eight stained-glass memorial windows. One is a fine example of early Tiffany glass, and another, a tribute to the distinguished clergyman-botanist-musician Moses Ashley Curtis, shows Jesus wearing an eighteenth-century hat encircled with the traditional crown of thorns. The most recent window was originally in the chapel at Fairntosh (Durham, 1804) and was given to St. Matthew's by the descendants of Duncan Cameron and Rebecca Benehan Cameron. The chapel no longer exists.

St. Matthew's Episcopal Church is on the National Register of Historic Places.

210 East King.

ST. MATTHEW'S CHURCHYARD

St. Matthew's Churchyard, with its specimen trees and flowering plants, is a place of serenity and beauty. Chief Justice Thomas Ruffin, and many members of the Ruffin, Graham, Collins,

St. Matthew's Episcopal Church (Rachel Best)

Cameron, Cain, Webb, and Strudwick families, are buried here.

In the east churchyard stands a memorial to the Reverend Moses Ashley Curtis, author, teacher, scientist, and clergyman. The bronze tablet, presented by the Hillsborough Historical Society, was dedicated April 25, 1970. Other rectors buried here are Dr. William D. Benton and the Reverend Robert C. Masterton. The first rector, the Reverend William Mercer Green, wanted to be buried here. However, he later became the first bishop of Mississippi and was buried in Jackson, Mississippi. His first wife and three children, "one who tarried not long enough to be named," are buried "very nearly beneath the altar" at St. Matthew's.

210 East King.

BELLEVUE (WEBB-MATHESON HOUSE)

Bellevue is a large 2½-story frame house situated on an expansive site overlooking St. Matthew's Church at the intersection of East Tryon and St. Mary's Road. It is built in the Italianate architecture, as evidenced by its third-story cupola and Corinthian columns.

Bellevue (Mary R. Cole)

The original east section was the home of James Phillips. In 1853 the estate was purchased by Thomas Blount Hill, who later added the west wing. The unique symmetry of this home is made complete by the eighty-foot-long porch across the entire front of the house. There are other enclosed porches opening from the dining room, west parlor, and master bedroom suite. The interior of the house is noted for its spacious rooms, six fireplaces, and fine panelling and moldings.

The original, separate brick kitchen house sits adjacent to the east courtyard. It is believed to be the oldest brick building still standing in Hillsborough. It contains a large cooking hearth and oven on the south end and an additional fireplace on the north side of the first level. There are two loft rooms and a fireplace upstairs. Some early cooking utensils still remain in this fine example of early detached kitchens.

209 East Tryon Street.

DICKERSON'S CHAPEL (A.M.E. CHURCH)

Dickerson's Chapel A.M.E. Church was originally the third Orange County Courthouse (1790). The building was sold to a Baptist minister, the Reverend Elias Dodson, after the fourth courthouse was completed in 1845. It has served as the First Baptist Church (organized November 19, 1853), a school for black children (operated by Pennsylvania Quakers), and a public school. The members

Dickerson's Chapel (H. G. Coleman, Jr.)

of Dickerson's Chapel (organized in 1851) bought the building in 1886.

Since 1891 the church has been extensively remodeled. It has been enlarged to the rear to form an apse, both a tower and a spire have been constructed, and the original frame building has been covered with brick (1947). However, visitors to the basement can still see the 1790 hand-hewn beams.

Southeast corner of Queen Street and Churton.

WILLIAM WHITTED HOUSE

The William Whitted House (ca. 1786), a private residence, served as the American Legion Hut for twenty-seven years. The southeast section facing Queen Street is the oldest part. A merchant, William Whitted, Jr., built the east room and hall. Sometime later an additional front room was built, and a second story with two bedrooms

William Whitted House

was added. A third section, the Churton Street wing, was built about 1840.

The parlor and central hall contain original doors with six-panels and beveled panelling. The well house, with its cone-shaped roof, is one of Hillsborough's most interesting secondary structures. The original wing has been repaired, both the house and well house have been roofed with cedar shakes, and the exterior has been repainted.

Northeast corner of Queen Street and Churton.

HEARTSEASE

Heartsease, a story-and-a-half Tidewater house, was owned by Mary ("Polly") Burke until 1837. The central portion was probably built by Sterling Harris (ca. 1786) although tradition says this wing was built by Polly Burke's father, Governor Thomas Burke. The house, named Heartsease by editor Dennis Heartt (1783–1870), has small dormer windows and an attic room allegedly occupied by an apprentice printer, William H. Holden, later a governor of North Carolina.

Heartsease remained in Dennis Heartt's family until 1988. It is now entered on the National Register of Historic Places.

113 East Queen Street.

THE WEBB HOUSE

The Webb House (1812) was originally a one-room schoolhouse built by Dr. James Webb, a founder of the North Carolina Medical Society. The school was operated by Governor Thomas Burke's daughter, Mary ("Polly") Burke, for the Webb children and their neighbors. It is believed that she had taught them in her home next door before she opened the school.

From the 1830s until 1983 the house was a private residence for successive generations of Dr. Webb's descendants, with the various families enlarging it to meet their needs. Over the years eight rooms have been added to the original log house, which is now the living room.

The interior, with ceilings that vary from high to low and windows in assorted sizes, is a study in contrasts. The exterior, too, is said to have "a mind of its own" and refuses to adhere to a specific architectural pattern. However, with its old brick walls, flanked by parallel rows of boxwoods, its well house and old-fashioned garden, this unique frame house is completely at home beside its colonial neighbor, Heartsease.

The property was sold to Harold and Marcia Grunewald in 1983. 117 East Queen Street.

The Webb House (Steven Garrison)

Mid-Lawn (Kevin Meredith, *News of Orange County*)

MID-LAWN

Mid-Lawn, a Victorian house near the intersection of Queen and Cameron streets, was built by James Webb, Jr., a grandson of Dr. James Webb.

When he bought the 2½-acre lot, Webb said, "I want to build the finest house in Hillsborough."

The house (1884) has porches on the east, west, and south sides. The west porch is enclosed. Interesting interior features include original ceiling medallions, crown moldings, and original wallpaper in the dining room and hall.

In 1919, the property was sold to David E. Patterson, Sr. Mrs. Patterson taught school for more than fifty years, fifteen as a kindergarten teacher in the little cottage on the northeast section of the lot.

131 East Queen Street.

Turner-Strudwick House (Kevin Meredith, *News of Orange County*)

TURNER-STRUDWICK HOUSE

William H. Phillips built the oldest portion of the Turner-Strud-- wick house before 1853. The dwelling, soon acquired by Phillips' business partner, Josiah Turner, was originally built on a five-acre block bounded on the north by East Orange, on the east by the old town limits (now North Cameron), on the south by East Union, and on the west by North Churton.

On August 16, 1889 the old Turner place was sold to Edmund Strudwick of Norfolk, Virginia. He was the elder son of Dr. William Strudwick, a well-known Hillsborough physician, and the brother of Shepperd Strudwick, Sr. He removed four rooms from the original structure, relocated them on an adjacent lot, and turned the dwelling 90 degrees. He also added four rooms to the front and an "L" to the back. In 1947 and 1948 two porches were removed because they were in need of repair and lumber had been difficult to get during World War II. A stoop was built over the north entrance, and the upstairs porch was removed. The south porch was left standing, but the railings were replaced with a different type. The house was repaired and completely repainted. When some sills were replaced, it was discovered that those under the original house had been hand-hewn and mortised with pegs.

Sheriff L. B. Lloyd purchased the property in 1922, and it remained in his family until 1979, when Dr. Michael Murphy bought the house from Frank Frederick and Mrs. Frederick (Sheriff Lloyd's granddaughter). He sold it to Clifford and Barbara Younger in 1984.

404 North Churton Street.

TAMARIND

Tamarind was built by Shepperd Strudwick (1868–1961) in 1903. The house, which has some Gothic features, was designed by Ralph Adams Cram, an ecclesiastical architect who designed the Cathedral of St. John the Divine. He was Susan Read Strudwick's brother-in-law.

The acre lot has an old-fashioned garden to the south, and a mammoth hydrangea and wisteria which defies control at the front. Pecans and aged beech have been saved by tree surgery.

318 North Churton Street.

TOWN HALL (RUFFIN-ROULHAC HOUSE)

The Town Hall, formerly the Ruffin-Roulhac House (ca. 1803), is the Hillsborough municipal building. In 1846 newspaper editor Dennis Heartt declared that Orange County's courthouse ". . . is perhaps not surpassed in the Union." Approximately 130 years later, then-mayor Fred Cates paraphrased Heartt's words and called the Ruffin-Roulhac House "the finest town hall in America." Today the restored former residence is now the town office building. The old dining room serves as the mayor's office; the former kitchen is the tax office; the food larder is a bathroom; and the conservatory houses plants.

The secondary buildings have also been restored. Chief Justice Thomas Ruffin's law office (his last one) is now the home of the Hillsborough Historical Society, and work on the milk house, the old servants quarters, the carriage house, and the water tower has been completed. Like all of Hillsborough's restored buildings, these will be used for various town services.

Fred Cates (re-elected mayor in 1987) got the idea for purchasing and restoring the property in 1971 after learning that the Nash-Hooper house was not available. The project, begun by a grant of $83,000 matched by the town, and supported with subsequent gifts and grants, cost almost $250,000. On July 6 and 7, ten months after work on the project began, the Town Hall employees were able to occupy their offices. Final work on the secondary

Town Hall (Ruffin-Roulhac House) (Steven Garrison)

buildings was completed in 1976, and dedication cermonies were held April 23, 1976.

Most of the furnishings, the light fixtures, and the plants have been contributed by townspeople and friends from other places. It is appropriate that the building should be Hillsborough's municipal hall.

Hillsborough's Town Hall is on the National Register of Historic Places.

101 East Orange Street.

SANS SOUCI

Sans Souci is believed to have been built by William Cain as a town house around 1801.

The original house, consisting of one central block with flanking wings, contained a hall and three rooms downstairs and two rooms upstairs. The hall, large downstairs room, and the larger upstairs room have very fine panelling and dentil molding. The panelling in the other original rooms is simpler.

It is believed that Dr. Pride Jones, son-in-law of William Cain, had the house remodeled during the second quarter of the nineteenth century. At this time, the front stoop was replaced with a porch, additional rooms were added at the rear of the house, the fireplace in the large downstairs room was moved from the east wall to the north wall, the roof line at the rear of the house was changed, and dormers were added.

John Berry may have done the remodeling for Dr. Jones. The back stairway, added at this time, closely resembles the one Berry designed in the Old Courthouse.

There are eight mantels in the house and each is a different design. In addition to the ten rooms on the main floors of the house, there are seven rooms—and four fireplaces—in the basement.

Although the original tract of land on which Sans Souci stands contained two hundred or more acres, there are only ten acres in the present tract. Also on the property are an outside kitchen, an office purportedly used by Drs. William Cain and Pride Jones as a medical office, and a small dwelling at one time used as a home for house servants.

Sans Souci was at one time the summer home of Episcopal bishop Theodore B. Lyman. He sold the house to Miss Jennie L. Hurton in 1893. Miss Hurton was governess to the Lyman children. After she came to live in Hillsborough, she married Sterling Ruffin, a son of Chief Justice Thomas Ruffin.

Mrs. Ruffin died in 1934. She bequeathed the house and contents to Samuel T. Latta, Jr. The present owners, H. Carlton McKee and H. Carlton McKee, Jr., are nephew and great-nephew of the late Mr. Latta. Some of the furniture owned by Mrs. Ruffin remains in the house.

Sans Souci is on the National Register of Historic Places.

237 East Corbin Street.

Sans Souci (Thomas C. Wagstaff)

BURWELL SCHOOL

The Burwell School (ca. 1821), "A Restoration Project for the Historic Hillsborough Commission," was a Presbyterian school for young ladies from 1837 to 1857. It was operated by Reverend Robert Burwell and Mrs. Burwell, both Virginia natives.

The south wing, originally a two-story dwelling with four rooms, was probably built by William Adams about 1821. In 1848 local architect John Berry added the north wing and altered the original section. He also realigned the house to face Churton Street instead of Union. The renovations made by a later owner have been removed, and the house is much as it was in 1848.

A kitchen and a necessary house—both brick—remain. They are attributed to John Berry. The other secondary buildings, including Burwell's office, are gone.

Burwell School is on the National Register of Historic Places. 319 North Churton Street.

PILGRIM'S REST (HASELL-NASH HOUSE)

Pilgrim's Rest, or the Hasell-Nash House, resembles the Semple House in Williamsburg. Both were evidently built from a model illustrated in Plate 37 of Robert Morris's book, *Rural Architecture*. The house has three pedimented units: a two-and-a-half-story central block with two lower wings. In 1943 the house was restored. At that time the west wing was enlarged, a fireplace like the one in the east wing was added, and the Gothic window in the central block was replaced with a Palladian window. Other renovations included replacing the plastering, laying a brick terrace at the back, and adding a new kitchen. Distinctive features include a fine stairway, horizontal panelling, and reeded mantels.

In 1974 Dr. and Mrs. H. W. Moore sold the house to Dr. and Mrs. Alexander Heard, who sold it to Dr. and Mrs. Thomas H. Cameron in 1979.

The house is listed in the National Register of Historic Places. 116 West Queen Street.

Pilgrim's Rest (Hasell-Nash House)

BERRY BRICK HOUSE

The Berry Brick House, once attributed to John Berry, was probably built by Samuel Hancock. (The building may have been built in 1805, and Berry was only seven.)

Brick was rarely used in Hillsborough before 1814, and the builder was apparently inexperienced. When building flat arches, he appeared to chip the bricks to make them fit. His use of a pointed brick for the keystone of the front door is an example. This brick was used in later buildings with which he was evidently associated.

The Berry Brick House was built for John Berry's mother, and it is possible John became interested in building while he watched Hancock at work. Although there are no records of when he decided to become an architect-builder, it is known that John Berry worked with Hancock later, and that he learned his trade well.

Berry Brick House (Thomas C. Wagstaff)

The house, the oldest brick dwelling in the original town limits, was sold by Berry's descendants in 1936 and restored by Dr. and Mrs. Furman McLarty between then and 1943. It was enlarged during that time, and the porch was removed. Mr. and Mrs. Ross Porter purchased the house in 1943 and made additional improvements. The present owners, Cdr. and Mrs. Charles Trumbull, bought the house in 1988 and have made further renovations.

The boxwoods that once flanked the walk at the front now envelop it. The well house is a copy of an earlier one.

208 West Queen Street.

ASHE HOUSE

The Ashe House is a two-story white frame house with Greek Revival features. It was probably built ca. 1840 by descendants of Governor Samuel Ashe. Henry N. Brown, a merchant-real estate investor, purchased the property in 1850 and sold it to Robert Faucett (Faucette) in 1859. It remained in his family until the Reverend Samuel Nicks bought it in 1945, when he retired from the Methodist ministry. It was later owned by Foy and Stella Nicks Bartlett (daughter of Reverend Nicks).

Michael Rierson, the present owner, began renovations in 1982 and has been rewarded with a sign on the front lawn identifying the house as old and historical and making it the first Hillsborough building to be placed on the National Register of Historic Places in several years.

Rierson found the house in "modest disrepair" and has redone some walls and ceilings, replaced wiring and plumbing, repaired chimneys, and done some landscaping and planting—particularly fruit trees.

Two previous additions doubled the size of the house, but it still

Ashe House (Thomas C. Wagstaff)

has many original items, including hand-milled six-inch oak flooring planks and the latticework around the porch.
144 North Wake Street.

UNITED METHODIST CHURCH

The United Methodist Church is a handsome white-trimmed brick
building designed and built by John Berry (ca. 1859). The original
frame structure was located on East Tryon Street on property purchased from Dr. James Webb in 1823.

The present church, which resembles the Old Courthouse, also a
Berry building, has tall windows and a distinctive tower and stee-
ple. Outstanding interior features include a gallery, the original
pulpit, and antique pews.
West Tryon Street.

NASH-HOOPER HOUSE

General Francis Nash built the high front block of the Hooper
House in 1772, but the rear wing may have been built earlier,
probably by Governor William A. Tryon's secretary, Isaac Edwards. (Nash, for whom Nashville, Tennessee, was named, was
mortally wounded at the Battle of Germantown, October 4, 1777.)

William Hooper, one of North Carolina's three signers of the
Declaration of Independence, bought the house in 1781. It remained in the Hooper family for seventy-two years. Later it was the
home of Governor William A. Graham. During the nineteenth
century, extensive alterations were made.

The house is the setting for several scenes in Inglis Fletcher's
Carolina novels, *The Wind in the Forest* and *Queen's Gift*. Over the
years it has been restored by successive owners.

In 1933 Charles and Adelaide Rosemond sold the house to Herman and Roberta Brown. During the 1950s the Browns restored
the east living room and renovated the kitchen, which has a distinctive flagstone hearth. Drs. Alfred and Mary Claire Engstrom
cleaned and cemented the cellar, re-roofed the house, and saved

Nash-Hooper House (Thomas C. Wagstaff)

some valuable old trees. Mr. and Mrs. Cecil Sanford have furnished it with many unusual objects acquired during his years as a U.S. foreign service officer.

The central block of the house is set on a stone foundation and has a central hall with a lateral back stair hall. The north wing, on the other hand, is a saddlebag with a log base. Although alterations have been made, the basic structure of the house, a fine example of Piedmont architecture, remains virtually unchanged.

Nash-Hooper House is both a National Historic Landmark and listed in the National Register of Historic Places.

118 West Tryon Street.

ROULHAC-HAMILTON HOUSE

The Roulhac-Hamilton House (ca. 1840) stands on a lot once owned by Edmund Fanning. It was the first home of the Roulhac family, who came to Hillsborough from Bertie County. The property was later owned by Major Daniel Heyward Hamilton.

Although the two-story house (originally frame) has been re-modeled and brick-veneered, its basic structure has been retained. The property is particularly noted for its bald cypress trees, grown from seed (ca. 1857), and its outstanding collection of English box.
147 West Tryon Street.

SCOTT HOUSE

The site of the Scott House, once part of Edmund Fanning's vast estate, may have previously belonged to Colonel Thomas Hart. Fanning, according to the 1769 purchase deed, built a "mansion house" on the lot, but the present house appears to have been constructed later (early 1800s). In 1817 Mary Cameron Anderson, Duncan Cameron's widowed sister, bought the house and lot from James Thompson, probably its builder. She and her two sons lived there until sometime after 1825.

The late Julius Scott bought the house in 1906. Present owners are his son Curtis and Mrs. Scott.

Scott House (Keith Coleman)

Interesting features of the house include end chimneys, an enclosed stairway, and wide horizontal panelling. It may originally have had dormer windows.

121 West Tryon Street.

PRESBYTERIAN CHURCH

The Presbyterian Church stands near the site of the first St. Matthew's (then a Church of England). The original hip roof and double-hung sash windows have been replaced, and the brick structure covered with cement. The tower and spire were added in 1892.

The Reverend John Knox Witherspoon, grandson of John Witherspoon (signer of the Declaration of Independence from New Jersey), organized the church and served as its first minister. It is the oldest Presbyterian church in continuous operation in North Carolina.

West Tryon Street.

THE OLD TOWN CEMETERY

In 1757 Lot 98 was laid out as "a public burying ground," with nine private cemeteries—all from Lot 97—being added sometime after 1846. These plots to the west of the original site were secured by deeds from Dr. William Hooper, a grandson of the signer of the Declaration of Independence. In the cemetery are a number of early graves which can no longer be identified and 184 with markers. William A. Graham (governor, secretary of the navy, Whig candidate for vice-president, and senator for both the Confederate States of America and the United States), Frederick Nash (chief justice), Archibald D. Murphey ("father of public education in North Carolina"), John Berry (architect-builder), and William Hooper (signer of the Declaration of Independence) are all buried here.

Churton Street and Tryon.

Presbyterian Church (Linda Kirby)

THE ORANGE COUNTY HISTORICAL MUSEUM

The Museum, founded by the Hillsborough Garden Club in 1956, had its public opening in 1958. Its prime purpose is to exhibit items depicting the life-styles and history of Orange County from the period of the Indians through 1865. Since 1983 it has been located in the Confederate Memorial Building. Items on display include Indian artifacts and a diorama of an Indian village, collections of early china and glass, silver pieces crafted by local artisans, antique firearms, and Civil War items. There is also a set of copper and brass standard weights and measures which Orange County imported from England in 1760.

The Museum is supported through the sale of historical books, maps, and pamphlets and by voluntary contributions. It is open daily (except Monday) 1:30 to 4:30 P.M. Sunday, Tuesday, Thursday, Friday, and Saturday, and 12:30 to 4:30 P.M. Wednesday.

201 North Churton Street.

THE CRAFT HOUSE

The Hillsborough Crafts Group operates a craft house. Items featured include facsimiles of early handicrafts made by area craftsmen.

The Craft House has been moved from the rear of the Burwell School to the basement of the Confederate Memorial Building.

201 North Churton Street.

MOUNT BRIGHT BAPTIST CHURCH

In 1866, shortly after the emancipation of slaves in the South, a number of Hillsborough's black citizens faced religious freedom for the first time. That year they organized a local Baptist church, later named Mount Bright after its first pastor, Reverend Alfred E. Bright.

The first church building was located on the Eno River near the south end of Churton Street. Later the church body moved to a place on Union Street, the home of the late Brother Louis Jenkins,

Mount Bright Baptist Church (H. G. Coleman, Jr.)

and on a site approximately three hundred yards from the present building. A third church was destroyed by fire in 1903.

Susan Graham, the widow of former Governor William A. Graham, donated the site for the fourth building, erected in 1906. In 1978–1979 the present church was built adjacent to the 1906 structure.

Union Street.

MASONIC HALL

The Masonic Hall (1823) belongs to Eagle Lodge 19 A.F. and A.M. chartered in 1791. The red brick Greek Revival structure was designed by state architect William Nichols and is believed to have been built by John Berry. The building, almost a perfect cube, has three bay windows on each side, and the white portico is supported

Masonic Hall (H. G. Coleman, Jr.)

by Ionic columns. Before it was remodeled, it had a gallery with an observatory and telescope.

Once called "the King Street Opera House," the building was unofficially the town's meeting hall. Located on Lot 23 on or near the site where colonial official Edmund Fanning's "fine house" was cut from its sills on September 25, 1770, it is one of the state's outstanding lodges. It is on the National Register of Historic Places.

King Street.

SAMUEL GATTIS HOUSE

The Samuel Gattis House, overlooking the historic Colonial Inn, was built in approximately 1906 by a prominent Hillsborough lawyer, judge, solicitor, and speaker of the North Carolina House of Representatives. Samuel M. Gattis moved to Hillsborough in the mid-1880s and constructed the house several years later after marrying Margaret P. ("Me Ma") Parish.

The Samuel Gattis House sits amidst large maple and pecan trees on 1.3 acres, including an area behind the Masonic Lodge which adjoins the property on the east. The house was built on the original site of one of Hillsborough's oldest homes (no longer standing), which was moved to the front corner of the property when the new house was constructed.

A notable feature of the property is the hexagon-shaped well house. The eighteenth-century well is one of the town's originals. It was actively used until a town water system was installed in the 1930s. From 1906 until the advent of a public water supply, water was pumped from the well into the house for use in the house's indoor plumbing system. The well house was restored in 1963 according to its original design.

The Samuel Gattis House features Edwardian-style architecture and has undergone no additions or exterior modifications since construction. A large, prominent porch graces the front of the house, for many years serving as a popular gathering place for passers-by. Today the porch is used frequently for entertaining

The Samuel Gattis House (Frank Sheffield)

and as a relaxed place to observe the many visitors to the Colonial Inn. Inside, the house features a large central hallway, heart-pine floors, original Victorian light fixtures, and seven working fireplaces, four of which are designed to burn coal and each with its original early twentieth-century ceramic tilework.

Of particular note is that the house has had only three owners since it was built. Following her husband's death in 1931, "Me Ma" Gattis lived in the house until her death in 1949. Members of the Gattis family occupied the house until 1963, when it was sold to W. Britton Sawyer. The current owners, former Hillsborough mayor Frank Sheffield and his wife, Roxanne, purchased the house in 1980.

158 West King Street.

COLONIAL INN

Lot 15, site of the Colonial Inn, was originally owned by county official Colonel Edmund Fanning. According to tradition, a tavern has stood here since the late 1700s. The lobby and east dining room of the present inn are in the old wing. The west wing and annex were added much later. The porch dining room, now enclosed, was originally the innyard.

Other names for the Colonial Inn have been Spencer's Tavern, Orange Hotel, Occoneechee Hotel, and Corbinton Inn.

153 West King Street.

TWIN CHIMNEYS

Twin Chimneys is a pre-Revolutionary house used as the setting for much of the novel *Joscelyn Cheshire*, by Sara Beaumont Kennedy (Doubleday and Page, 1901).

The most distinctive features of the exterior are the huge twin chimneys on the east and west sides. The interior has beaded weatherboarding, pine wainscoting, and fine mantels. The three original dormer windows have been removed, the portico replaced by a porch, and the once separate kitchen is now connected to the

Twin Chimneys (Steven Garrison)

house. The panelling in the hall came from the Nash-Kollock
school, a pre-Revolutionary dwelling demolished in 1947.

168 West King Street.

THE INN AT TEARDROP

Lot 18, on West King Street, has been associated with inns off and
on throughout its long history. It was owned by Edmund Fanning
until he sold it to Thomas King, an innkeeper, in 1768. The main
body of the present structure is probably King's old inn.

Notable eighteenth-century owners include General Thomas
Person, Peter Malett, William Duffy, and John Taylor, who was
clerk of the Superior Court from 1800 to 1845.

In 1880 D. C. Parks acquired Lot 18 as well as Lot 15, the Colonial Inn, and turned all six buildings into the Occoneechee Hotel.

During the early 1900s, the house served intermittently as an inn and a private residence. In 1937 the J. W. Richmond family bought the property and re-opened the house as a private residence. They later moved the old kitchen-dining room wing, which was separate from the house, to Wake Street and converted it into a small house.

In 1986 Tom Roberts bought the property and re-opened the house, after extensive renovations, as the Inn at Teardrop, a bed and breakfast. The name comes from the teardrop-shaped windows on the front doors and the molding around the eaves of the house.

175 West King Street.

The Inn at Teardrop (Thomas C. Wagstaff)

First Baptist Church (Quentin Patterson)

FIRST BAPTIST CHURCH

The First Baptist Church (1860–1870) is a brick building of Romanesque design with a freestanding tower to the north. Completion was delayed because of the Civil War.

Inside, the structure is designed with a high open ceiling and exposed hand-carved beams. The Romanesque arch is used extensively throughout the interior. During the early years there was a pointed spire on top of the tower, but it was removed about 1923 because it had deteriorated. In 1952 the church launched a movement to erect the Educational Building and to improve the Sanctuary and grounds. Ten years later a brick parsonage was built on

West King Street. During 1976 plans were inaugurated to expand and renovate the Educational Building. The new facility was dedicated in the spring of 1977. In November 1978, a new spire was built, with a cross at the top.

Corner of Wake and West King streets.

PETER BROWNE RUFFIN HOUSE (RUFFIN-SNIPES)

The old front section of the Peter Browne Ruffin House, constructed by an unknown builder, resembles William Courtney's Yellow House. The dining room, most likely a one-room house, was carted from Alamance County.

Beaded weatherboarding, narrow windows, and end chimneys are interesting features. Local architect John Berry altered and remodeled the house for Peter Browne Ruffin, probably during the 1840s. The interior includes a number of details from New England architect Asher Benjamin's books, with his distinctive acanthus leaf design appearing on the stairway.

320 West King Street.

PATTERSON-PALMER HOUSE

The Patterson-Palmer House stands near the intersection of Margaret Lane and Wake Street. The one-and-a-half-story frame structure, restored since 1960, has high ceilings, fine mantels, and a lateral hall. (The only other such hall is at Ayr Mount.) The dormer windows on the north, removed before 1905, have been restored. The house is named for James Patterson and Postmaster James Palmer.

173 West Margaret Lane.

THE NASH LAW OFFICE ("STUDIO")

The Nash Law Office is now the property of the Hillsborough Historical Society, Inc. The older section, the east wing, was probably built by Francis Nash between 1768 and 1772. It served as the law office of Duncan Cameron from 1801 to 1807 and of Chief

Justice Frederick Nash from 1807 to 1858. Following Nash's death in 1858 it became a part of the Nash-Kollock School, operated from 1859 until the 1890s by his spinster daughters, Sally and Maria, and their cousin, Miss Sarah Kollock. The office was used as a music room. In 1863 the two west rooms, "Cousin Sarah's rooms," were added.

The steep-roofed structure is a representative Hillsborough law office. The original wing retains its six-panelled doors and beveled panelling. Both the weatherboarding and the panelled floors are in random widths. The reeded mantel, so common in Hillsborough, may have been added later. The front porch was apparently added in the 1930s and the small kitchen and bath on the south side after 1942. The house, for many years a private residence, has an old-fashioned garden on the south.

The Nash Law Office is on the National Register of Historic Places.

143 West Margaret Lane.

The Nash Law Office (Mary R. Cole)

Burnside (Elisabeth Stagg)

BURNSIDE

Burnside was once a part of the 253-acre estate owned by James Hogg (1729–1805), a Scotsman and a partner in the Transylvania Company that helped open up the West. Thomas Ruffin, a future chief justice, purchased the property in 1811. He lived in a one-story frame house (no longer standing) which was probably built by James Hogg.

The present two-and-one-half-story house is believed to have been built by Thomas Ruffin's son-in-law, Paul Carrington Cameron. The now enlarged house has many distinctive features, including original doors with six-panels and moldings unlike any others in Hillsborough. Some doors have HL-hinges, and a number have English rim locks. Both the old kitchen and the octagonal-shaped ice pit are brick. The estate, often called Cameron Park, has many specimen trees.

Thomas Ruffin's Law Office (the first one he acquired) remains. It is a one-room frame building with random-width pine floors, original beaded weatherboarding, and a single fireplace. There are four windows: two each on the north and south sides. The building, which rests on a foundation of native stone, is smaller than most law offices.

Entrance at east end of Margaret Lane.

POPLAR HILL (POPLAR LODGE OR OCCONEECHEE FARM)

Poplar Hill, a typical two-story Piedmont farmhouse, was originally built in 1794 on James Hogg's 1,100-acre tract south of the Eno

Poplar Hill (Thomas C. Wagstaff)

River called Occoneechee Farm. It was passed on to his daughter, Robina, and then to her son, John Wall Norwood.

In the 1890s General Julian S. Carr purchased the tract, remodeled the house, and the property became a model farm. It was also a place which sold bottled mineral water secured from a spring on the farm and where Indian arrowheads and other artifacts were often found.

But a tornado in 1919 destroyed two barns, damaged a third, killed live stock, and destroyed giant oaks and fruit trees. Only the house managed to escape the twister. For many reasons, Occoneechee Farm was sold in 1923.

In 1980 a later owner sold the house—slated for demolition—and it was moved across the Eno River to its present location. It is difficult to determine how much of Hogg's original construction remains. James Freeland moved and renovated it.

Burnside Drive.

MONTROSE

Governor William Graham purchased this property from the Kirkland estate. The present house was built by Major John Graham in 1898 and remodeled in 1948. Two earlier houses were destroyed by fire.

East King Street Extension.

AYR MOUNT

Ayr Mount (ca. 1800–1815), built by William Kirkland of Ayr, Scotland, has often been called "the finest house in the Hillsborough area." The brick house, designed with a high central block and flanking wings, has large-scale rooms, high ceilings, and a lateral hall. (The only other such hall in Hillsborough is at the Patterson-Palmer House.) West of the house lies the old family cemetery.

Although the exact construction date of Ayr Mount is not known, letters William Kirkland wrote to his son-in-law, Chief Justice Thomas Ruffin, in December 1815, state that the house was nearly complete at that time. According to Kirkland family tradition, it took twelve years to build the house, and construction may have been interrupted during the War of 1812.

The bricks used in the construction were made from clay dug on the property, and the wood used for panelling is believed to have come from trees cut on the site. Ayr Mount remained in the Kirkland family until 1985, when it was purchased and restored by financier Richard H. Jenrette.

Before the colors used in repainting the interior were selected, George Fore of Raleigh analyzed the original colors, and those used in repainting were matched exactly to the original ones.

Although all of the original outbuildings are gone, the family cemetery contains a priceless record of successive generations of the Kirklands. The Eno River—visible during the fall and winter—lies southeast of the house.

Ayr Mount is listed on the National Register of Historic Places. St. Mary's Road.

Ayr Mount (Quentin Patterson)

SUNNYSIDE

Sunnyside, an early house, was bought and remodeled by architect John Berry (ca. 1844). Material from the original Methodist Church, a frame building on East Tryon Street, was used to build the dining room which was added about fifteen years later.

The frame dwelling has eight rooms and a Palladian window. The panelling and stair brackets are from Asher Benjamin's pattern books. The front porch Berry built has been replaced by one with columns, and the famous elm grove that once surrounded the house is gone.

Approximately 2.5 miles from town on St. Mary's Road.

Sunnyside (Mark Gordon)

Maple Hill (courtesy Mrs. D. Hollandsworth)

MAPLE HILL

Maple Hill, an enlarged and restored eighteenth-century dwelling, is located on St. Mary's Road. The eight-room frame structure, now "H"-shaped, stands on a wooded hill. Surrounding it are green acres complemented by maples, box, and old-fashioned flowers. At the rear of the house, there is an old kithen with hand-hewn ceiling beams, a huge fireplace, and an unusual herb garden near the door.

Mr. and Mrs. D. E. Hollandsworth purchased Maple Hill in 1949. The property, almost sixty-four acres, is part of a 381-acre tract granted by John Earl Granville to James Taylor in 1753. Tradition says there was once a government-licensed distillery on the creek, and that the house was a lookout for Indians.

When the Hollandsworths moved to Maple Hill, they found a trapdoor in the kitchen, and were told the cook had slept above it. They also learned that at one time food had been carried across the courtyard and put through a window onto a shelf in the dining room.

In restoring the house, they had to remove an upstairs window because there was a musket hole below it. They also discovered a message etched on a pane of glass (broken during restoration) that read, "Goodbye Maple Hill, in the spring I will see you again."

2.9 miles NE on St. Mary's Road.

ST. MARY'S CHAPEL AND CHURCHYARD

The original St. Mary's Chapel—one of the first Anglican churches in the area—was erected in the northeast corner of what is now St. Mary's Cemetery. It was a log structure on a one-acre plot believed to have been donated by Thomas Holden. The native stones used for the foundation may be seen at the original site.

In 1859 the congregation bought an adjoining tract and built a brick church. The structure cost $2,000, and according to tradition, the bricks were made in a field by laborers employed by Polly White, a strong supporter of the chapel.

During the 1930s, services were discontinued except for the annual Homecoming Service, started in 1952 by the St. Mary's Grange and now supported by the Friends of the Chapel. Since 1975—when restoration plans were finalized—the wall and ceiling structures have been secured, the brick walls pointed up, the buttresses restored, and the flooring replaced with old lumber (except at the altar, where the flooring is original).

The walls were replastered and crumbled again because of seepage through the original handmade bricks. In 1988—because waterproofing was ineffective—a moisture barrier was installed over the crumbling plaster, and a sheetrock wall was added.

In 1972 the North Carolina Department of Archives and History approved a Highway Historical Marker for the Chapel. The following inscription directs people to a simple brick church with a high open ceiling supported by hand-hewn beams:

St. Mary's Chapel
Established as Anglican Chapel
ca. 1759. Present building
constructed in 1859, stands
500 ft. N.

St. Mary's Road.

St. Mary's Chapel (H. G. Coleman, Jr.)

Chatwood (The Coach House) (Tony Rumple, *Durham Morning Herald*)

CHATWOOD (THE COACH HOUSE)

The history of Chatwood is, to a large extent, traditional. The structure is actually two houses of about the same age. The east section is on its original site; the west wing is the Naile Johnson house, which first stood east of Hillsborough.

The original house was an inn, which is why the house is still sometimes called the Coach House. It was probably built by Robert Faucette about 1790. The road in front of the house, sometimes called the King's Highway, is an ancient road from Oxford (or Harrisburg) to Salisbury. A few hundred yards west of the house, it crosses the Eno River by a ford just south of Faucette's Mill. A similar house once stood on the west side of the river. These inns provided lodging for travelers when the Eno was too full to ford.

About 1900 the house had several owners and, for a while, was used as an elementary school. In 1937 the Vernon Altvaters bought the property, and except for the addition of modern heating and plumbing facilities, restored it to almost its original condition. The out-buildings, the kitchen, and the necessary house, however, disappeared long ago.

About 1938 the west wing, only a shell, was added. Dr. and Mrs. Charles Blake finished the interior: the first floor as a studio, and the second as a study, a dressing room, and a bath. They also remodeled the kitchen, added a screened porch, and installed a bathroom for the east bedroom on the second floor.

At one time water was brought up by a "water boy," an arrangement of pulleys which moved a bucket from a spring in a small branch west of the house. Almost certainly the bucket had to be filled by hand.

Distinctive features of Chatwood include random-width pine floors, side walls, ceilings, and panelled mantels. The spacious lawn has an herb garden, a fine collection of old roses, and a spring garden noted for its perennials.

Chatwood is on the National Register of Historic Places.

0.8 miles west on Highway 70; right 2 miles on Faucette Mill Road.

THE COMMANDANT'S HOUSE

The Commandant's House, built in 1859, is all that remains of the Hillsborough Military Academy. One of two such schools in operation in North Carolina when the Civil War began, it was the home of Colonel Charles Tew, who started the academy on January 12, 1859. The Barracks, which housed 150 cadets, stood to the west.

The two-story house, said to have been built from bricks made on the site, has solid brick walls seventeen inches thick, and a tower at each corner, making it resemble a castle. The interior has tall narrow windows, high ceilings, and wide floorboards. The front

The Commandant's House (Thomas C. Wagstaff)

room windows have offset corners that may have been gun port or turret spaces. The house, located beyond the town limits on Barracks Road, has been a private residence since 1965.

The Commandant's House is on the National Register of Historic Places.

Barracks Road.

MOOREFIELDS

Moorefields (1785), a two-story frame house, is designed with a high central block and flanking right-angle wings. Built by U.S. Supreme Court justice Alfred Moore as a summer residence, the house has the only remaining Chinese Chippendale staircase in the area (the other, at Lochiel, was destroyed by fire).

Approximately 3.5 miles from the Old Courthouse on Dimmock's Mill Road.

Eno Lodge (Quentin Patterson)

ENO LODGE (NORWOOD OR THE EAGLES' NEST)

Eno Lodge, the site of Lord Cornwallis's second encampment, stands on a 13.5-acre tract overlooking the Dark Walk and the Eno River. The two-story white frame dwelling has been altered and enlarged, but the front section was built in 1825.

Eno Lodge was named by Judge Lancaster Bailey, who bought the estate from John C. Norwood in 1848. Mrs. Bailey loved gardens and employed the Lindley Nurseries in Greensboro to landscape the grounds. She also planned and laid out the gardens, and many of her plantings remain, including fine roses and a rock garden.

James E. Jones bought Eno Lodge from Malthias Manley in 1880 and left it to his brother Clarence D. Jones in 1900. The present owner is Clarence D. Jones, Jr.

South Churton Street Extension.

HIGHLANDS

Highlands is a rambling two-story white house on a five-acre site. The two west rooms are constructed of logs (ca. 1844) and were used as a school.

Highway 70-A East.

OVER THE RIVER

Over the River is a two-story frame house standing on a twenty-acre site on the south bank of the Eno. The first four rooms were built ca. 1820–1825.

Highway 70-A East.

THE GATEWOOD HOUSE

George Washington slept at the Whit Gatewood House near Yanceyville on June 3, 1791, but if he returned to the site now, he would not find the frame dwelling. Instead, he would have to travel to Hillsborough, where the old house—now restored—has stood since 1978 (moved and renovated by James Freeland).

Washington's brief stop came during his famous "southern tour," which began in Philadelphia on March 21, 1791, and ended in mid-June after a visit to Maryland, Virginia, the Carolinas, and Georgia. His visit to Gatewood is documented in a diary he kept during a sixty-eight-day, 1,700-mile trip through the South, where the president hoped to get acquainted with his constituents throughout the nation. He had announced his plans to visit every part of the country following his inauguration in 1789, and the Caswell County visit was his last stop in North Carolina before he crossed the line into Virginia.

The first president traveled in an ivory and gilt coach drawn by four horses, with the Washington coat of arms decorating the quarter panels. Accompanied by Governor Alexander Martin, he had visited Salem and Guilford, and it was raining when he breakfasted at the Troublesome ironworks, seventeen miles from Guilford. He suffered from rheumatism, and, because his information was incorrect, he had traveled on June 3 twelve miles further than he had intended "to one Gatewood within two miles of Dix' ferry over the Dan at least 30 miles from the Iron works." On Saturday, June 4, 1791, he breakfasted there, and, tradition says, picked a rose and stuck it in his buttonhole. That day's entry in his diary states: "Left Mr. Gatewood's about half after six o'clock—and between his house and the ferry passed the line which divides the States of No. Carolina and Virginia. . . ."

There is no marker in front of the restored house, and George Washington could not have slept at all the places he allegedly stayed. However, according to his diary, an entry written by his own hand states that he was at the Gatewood House June 3–4, 1791, and the item is included in the handwritten copy on file in the Library of Congress, Washington, D.C.

South Churton Street Extension.

The Gatewood House (H. G. Coleman, Jr.)

The Nathaniel Rochester House (Thomas C. Wagstaff)

THE NATHANIEL ROCHESTER HOUSE

The Rochester House, believed to have been the home of early General Assemblyman Nathaniel Rochester, has been renovated and enlarged. Douglas Harris, who became fascinated with historic places while restoring an old house in 1984, bought the property in December 1985.

The structure consists of the original two rooms (ca. 1785) and the additions, constructed from old wood and utilizing three of the five original chimneys. It covers approximately eighteen hundred square feet.

Rochester left North Carolina for Maryland and later moved to New York. Rochester, the city he founded, is named for him.

West King Street.

Conclusion

Hillsborough, long referred to as "the town Cornwallis would recognize," is going to grow more in the next twenty years than it has in the last two hundred. This means it is going to change more, also—a fact residents already note with apprehension when drought causes water restrictions, and the cars on Churton are backed up like a caravan of tortoises.

There were two celebrations held in the area during July and August 1988, however, which focused on the past and related it to the present. The reenactment of the Constitutional Convention of 1788 included three presentations of *The 12th Lantern*, a play based on actual events, and written by Nancy Wallace Henderson especially for the celebration.* On Saturday, there was a street carnival that centered around the Old Courthouse, where the appointed delegates of 1988 met (the convention of 1788 had met in the Old St. Matthew's—a Church of England—that burned ca. 1793).

The most moving part of the 1988 event was the spectators' awareness that James Iredell was a federalist because he believed in a strong government, and Willie Jones was an antifederalist because he feared what such a government could do *to* an individual more than he trusted what it could do *for* him. The animated sidewalk discussions, which also focused on current issues, showed clearly why the Bill of Rights *is* so important, and increased support for the antifederalists who would not ratify a constitution that did not consider individual rights.

The Eno-Occaneechi Indian powwow, held in nearby Mebane on August 12–13, also focused on individual participation in group activities. The events included dances and tepee and craft contests. There were 3,000 attendees from more than a dozen tribes, and many non-Indian observers. A powwow is a social and cultural gathering which promotes unity and tries to help the tribe regain some of the identity it has lost during several centuries.

When white settlers came to Orange County, they found a seventeenth-century Indian Trading Path that crossed the Eno River, probably at a point west of Hillsborough, and continued to the territory of the Catawba Indians near Salisbury and on to Augusta, Georgia. The first roads in the colony were Indian trails, which were usually the shortest, most desirable routes the tribes could follow. Because the rivers of the East were more important to the young colony than roads, it was not until 1755—a year after Hillsborough was platted—that a road between the Orange County Courthouse and Cape Fear was authorized.

However, since I-40 opened in November 1988, virtually all roads in North Carolina lead to Hillsborough, where a Constitutional Convention in 1788 demanded that a Bill of Rights be added before its delegates would ratify the Constitution of the United States. This section of our most prized document should help progressives and preservationists move toward a new century and still preserve the eighteenth century—Hillsborough, once called "the foremost town in the Back Country."

The reenactment dates were July 22, 23, 24.

Old Orange County Courthouse (Quentin Patterson)

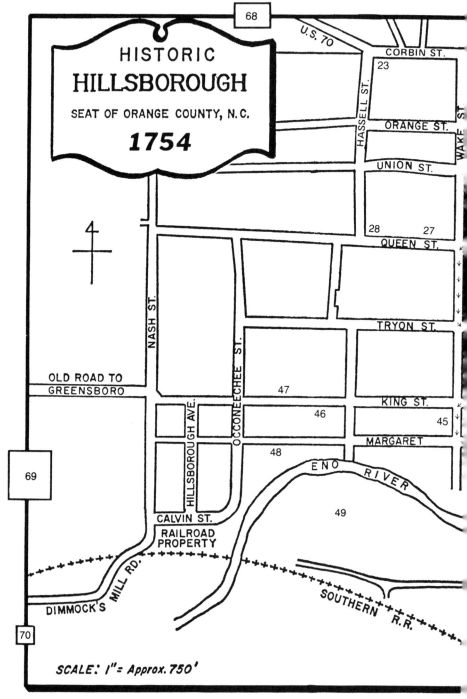

SCALE: 1" = Approx. 750'

This map is a publication of the Hillsborough Historical Society, and is reprinted with their permission.

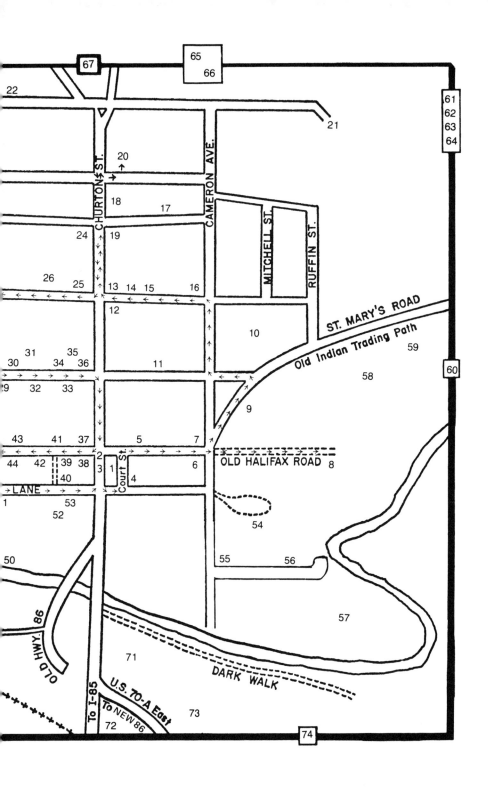

KEY TO MAP

Walking Tour Order   *Map Number*

Old Orange County Courthouse 1
Town Clock and Cupola 1
The Burke Marker 1
Churton Marker 3
Norwood-Jones Law Office 4
William Courtney's Yellow House 5
Dickson House 6
Seven Hearths 7
The Regulator Marker 8
St. Matthew's Episcopal Church and Churchyard 9
Bellevue 10
Dickerson's Chapel 12
William Whitted House 13
Heartsease 14
The Webb House 15
Mid-Lawn 16
Turner-Strudwick House 18
Tamarind 19
Town Hall (Ruffin-Roulhac House) 20
Sans Souci 21
Burwell School 24
Pilgrim's Rest (Hasell-Nash House) 26
Berry Brick House 27
Ashe House 29
United Methodist Church 30
Nash-Hooper House 31
Roulhac-Hamilton House 32
Scott House 33
Presbyterian Church 34
Old Town Cemetery 35
Orange County Historical Museum and
    Craft House 36
Mount Bright Baptist Church ..... No Map Key Number
Masonic Hall 41
Samuel Gattis House .... No Map Key Number
Colonial Inn 42
Twin Chimneys 43
The Inn at Teardrop 44
First Baptist Church 45

Peter Browne Ruffin House (Ruffin-Snipes) 47
Patterson-Palmer House 51
The Nash Law Office 52
Burnside 54
Poplar Hill 55
Montrose 58
Ayr Mount 59
Sunnyside 61
Maple Hill 62
St. Mary's Chapel and Churchyard 63
Chatwood (The Coach House) 68
The Commandant's House 69
Moorefields 70
Eno Lodge 71
Highlands 72
Over the River 73
The Gatewood House .... No Map Key Number
The Nathaniel Rochester
    House .... No Map Key Number

Appendix

Owners of houses in Hillsborough

Ashe House, Michael Rierson
Ayr Mount, Richard H. Jenrette
Bellevue (Webb-Matheson House), Vaughn and Margaret Haight
Berry Brick House, Cdr. and Mrs. Charles Trumbull
Burnside, Dr. and Mrs. Jay Weiss
Chatwood (the Coach House), Mrs. Ralph Watkins
Commandant's House, Mr. and Mrs. Lucius Cheshire, Sr.
William Courtney's Yellow House, Clinton Lindley
Eno Lodge, Clarence Jones
Gatewood House, James Freeland
Samuel Gattis House, Mr. and Mrs. Frank Sheffield
Heartsease, Mrs. Frances Phillips
Highlands, Elizabeth Collins
Mid-Lawn, Dr. and Mrs. Dirk Frankenberg
Montrose, Craufurd and Nancy Goodwin
Moorefields, Moorefields Foundation
Nash-Hooper House, Mr. and Mrs. Cecil Sanford
Over the River, Mr. and Mrs. Lucius Cheshire, Jr.
Patterson-Palmer House, Elizabeth Matheson
Pilgrim's Rest (Hasell-Nash House), Dr. and Mrs. Thomas H. Cameron
Poplar Hill, James Freeland

Peter Browne Ruffin House (Ruffin-Snipes), Mr. and Mrs. Jack Snipes

Nathaniel Rochester House, Douglas Harris

Roulhac-Hamilton House, Mr. and Mrs. John Roberts

Seven Hearths, Mr. and Mrs. Wallace Burt

Sunnyside, The Baldwin Family

Tamarind, Mr. and Mrs. John Kennedy, Jr.

Turner-Strudwick House, Clifford and Barbara Younger

Twin Chimneys, Mr. and Mrs. Paul Williams

Webb House, Harold and Marcia Grunewald

William Whitted House, Anne Needham Beere

Bibliography

HISTORIES

Coon, Charles Lee. *North Carolina Schools and Academies, 1790–1840, A Documentary History.* Raleigh: Edwards & Broughton, 1915.

Lefler, Hugh and Paul Wager (eds.). *Orange County, 1752–1952.* Chapel Hill: The Orange Printshop, 1953.

Lefler, Hugh Talmadge, and Newsome, Albert Ray. *North Carolina.* Chapel Hill: University of North Carolina Press, 1954.

Lloyd, Allen Alexander and Pauline O. *History of the Town of Hillsborough, 1754–1966.* Durham: 1966.

Nash, Francis. *Hillsborough, Colonial and Revolutionary.* Raleigh: Edwards & Broughton, 1903.

NEWSPAPERS AND PERIODICALS

Colton, Henry E. "Towns of the Revolution—Hillsborough, N.C." *Southern Hillsborough Literary Messenger,* Vol. XXIII, No. 3 (Sept. 1856), pp. 161–176.

Hillsborough Recorder, Weekly, February 8, 1820–1877.

Lacy, Allen. "The Wild Cyclamen of Montrose." *American Horticulture,* October 1985, pp. 26–29.

The State. Vol. XIV, October 5, 1946.

BIOGRAPHIES

Boyd, William K. "Dennis Heartt." An Annual Publication of Historical Papers. Series II (1898), pp. 34–41. Trinity College Historical Society.

Webb, Mena. *Jule Carr: General without an Army.* Chapel Hill: University of North Carolina Press, 1987.

BIBLIOGRAPHY

PUBLIC RECORDS

Miscellaneous papers. Orange County Clerk of Courts Office and Orange County
    Register of Deeds Office, Hillsborough, N.C.

BROCHURES

Eno Powwow Information, August 12–13, 1988, printed by the Eno Occaneechi
    Indian Association.
"Historic Hillsborough." Hillsborough Historical Society, Inc., 1977.
"Walking Tour, Historic Hillsborough." Hillsborough Historical Society, Inc., 1966
    and 1986.

UNPUBLISHED

Kennedy, John P., Jr. "Tamarind: History of a Hillsborough House." 1977.

Index

Adams, William, 75
Alamance, Battle of, 14, 40
Alamance County, 16, 38, 92
Albright, Dr. Frank P., 58
Altvater, Margaret ("Peggy") (Mrs. Vernon), 103
Altvater, Vernon, 103
A.M.E. Church (Dickerson's Chapel), 65–66
American Horticulturist, 48
American Legion Hut, 66
American Revolution, 14, 42, 62, 89
Anderson, General G. B., 44
Anderson, Mary Cameron, 81
Anderson, General Robert, 45
Antifederalists, 109
Architecture
  Edwardian-style, 87
  Georgian, 26
  Gothic, 26
  Gothic Revival, 17
  Greek Revival, 17
  Japanese, 26
  Piedmont, 17, 60, 80
  Spanish-Moorish-Texan, 26
  Tidewater, 17
  Tripartite, 17
  Victorian, 69, 88
Archives and History, Division of, 43

Artists, 26
Asbury, Bishop Francis, 60
Ashe House, 77
Ashe, Samuel, 77
Asheville, 44
Ayr Mount, 17, 92, 96, 97
Ayr, Scotland, 97

"Back Country," 13, 21, 110
Bailey, Judge Lancaster, 105
Bailey, Mrs. Lancaster, 105
Baptist, 65
Baptist Church, 65
Barnes, Rep. Anne, 43
Barracks, the, 33, 103
Bartlett, Foy, 78
Bartlett, Stella (Mrs. Foy), 78
Bellevue (Webb-Matheson House), 63, 64
Benjamin, Asher, 57, 92, 98
Bennett Place, 34, 42, 45
Bentonville, 34
Berry Brick House, 76–77
Berry, John, 55, 57, 62, 73, 75, 76, 79, 82, 85, 92, 98
Berry, Mrs. Rhoda, 76
Bertie County, 80
Bible, 38
Biddle, Mary Duke Foundation, 43
Bill of Rights, 15, 109

Blake, Dr. Charles, 42, 103
Blake, Helen M. (Helen Blake
    Watkins), 42, 103
Breckenridge, General J. C., 42
Bright, Rev. Alfred E., 84
Brown, Henry N., 77
Brown, Herman, 79
Brown, Roberta, 79
"Bucket brigade," 22
Burke, Mary ("Polly"), 67
Burke, Governor Thomas, 67
Burnside, 94, 95
Burwell, Margaret Anna
    Robertson (Mrs. Robert), 75
Burwell, Rev. Robert, 75
Burwell School, 31, 75, 84

Cabe, Barnaby, 60
Cadets, Hillsborough, 33
Cain, William, 73
California, 22
Cameron, Duncan, 62, 81
Cameron, Paul Carrington, 18, 44,
    45, 94
Cameron, Rebecca Benehan, 62
Cameron, Dr. Thomas H., 75
Cameron, Leigh (Mrs. Thomas
    H.), 75
Cape Fear River, 110
Carroll, Walter, 26
Cates, Frederick S., 71, 72
Cathedral of St. John the Divine,
    the, 71
"Central," 22, 23
Chapel Hill, 44, 50
Chatwood ("Coach House"), 102,
    103
Cheshire, James Webb, Sr., 46
Cheshire, Bishop Joseph Blount,
    Jr., 46
Cheshire, Lucius M., Sr., 34
Cheshire, Nellie Davis (Mrs. Lu-
    cius M.), 34
Childsburg, 13
Chippendale, Chinese, 17, 51, 104

Church of England, 58, 62, 82,
    101, 109
Churton, William, 13
Citadel, the, 33
Civil War, 34, 42, 43, 84, 91, 103
"Coach House" (Chatwood), 102,
    103
Coit, Frances Elizabeth, 38
Collins, Annie Cameron, 45
Collins, Elizabeth, 45
Collins, Paul Cameron, 45
Colonial Inn, 34, 88
Commandant's House, 34, 103–4
Confederate, 34, 42, 43, 45
Congress, Provincial, 15
Constitution, 15
Constitutional Convention, 15
Corbinton, 13
Corbinton Inn, 88
Cornwallis, Charles Lord, 15, 22,
    47
Courtney, William, 22, 23, 60
Courtney, William (House), 22–
    23, 60, 92
Craft House, 84
Cram, Ralph Adams, 26, 28, 71
Curtis, Moses Ashley, 39, 62, 63
Cyclamen, 48, 49

Daniel Morgan Register, 48
Dark Walk, 105
Davis, Jefferson, 42
Declaration of Independence, 79,
    82
Dickens, Charles, 47
Dickerson's Chapel (A.M.E.
    Church), 65, 66
Dickson House, 41–43, 60
Dodson, Rev. Elias, 65
Doric, 57
Dormer windows, 24, 26
Doubleday & Page, 88
Draper-Savage, Edward T., 51
Duffy, William, 89
Duke Foundation, 31

Duke University, 31, 48
Durham County, 47
Durham Methodist District, 29, 31
Durham Morning Herald, 26
Durham Station, 42

Eagle Lodge (Masonic Hall), 85, 86
East, 15, 110
Educational Building (Baptist Church), 91
Edwards, Isaac, 79
England, 58, 84
English, 35
Engstrom, Dr. Alfred, 79
Engstrom, Dr. Mary Claire (Mrs. Alfred), 79
Eno Lodge (Norwood or the Eagles' Nest), 105
Eno River, 45, 50, 61, 84, 95, 97, 102, 105
Evans, C. N. B. & Son, 36

Fairgrounds, 33
Fairntosh, 62
Fanning, Edmund, 80, 81, 86, 89
Faucette, Robert, 78, 102
Faucette's Mill, 102
Federal, 51
Federalists, 109
First Baptist Church, 17, 91, 92
Fletcher, Inglis, 79
Frederick, Frank, 71
Frederick, Jeanne Lloyd (Mrs. Frank), 71
Freeland, James, 45, 106

Gatewood House, 106, 107
Gatewood, Whit, 106, 107
Germantown, Battle of, 79
Goldsboro, 29
Goodwin, Craufurd, 48
Goodwin, Nancy (Mrs. Craufurd), 48, 49
Gordon, Major William, 34

Gordon, Mamie, 22, 23
Gordon, William, 22
Graham, Alexander H. ("Sandy"), Jr., 48
Graham, Alexander H. ("Sandy"), Sr., 48
Graham, James (Earl of Montrose), 47
Graham, John, 48
Graham, Major John W., 47
Graham, Kathleen Long (Mrs. A. H., Sr.), 48
Graham, Governor William A., 47, 48, 57
Granville, John Earl, 100
Great Hall, 51
Green, Bishop William Mercer, 63
Greensboro, 105
Grunewald, Harold, 68
Grunewald, Marcia (Mrs. Harold), 68
Guilford County, 16

Hamilton, Lily, 40
Hamilton, Major Daniel Heyward, 80
Hamilton, Nancy, 40
Hampton Court Palace (England), 28
Hampton, General Wade, 42, 43
Hardscrabble, 47
Harris, Douglas, 108
Harrisburg, 102
Hart, Colonel Thomas, 81
Hasell, Eliza G., 15
Hasell-Nash House ("Pilgrim's Rest"), 15, 75
"Haunted houses," 38, 39
Hawks, Francis Lister, 62
Hawks, John, 62
Heard, Dr. Alexander, 75
Heard, Mrs. Alexander, 75
Hearstease, 35, 67, 68
Heartt, Dennis, 35, 36, 37, 55, 67, 71

Heartt, Edwin, 36
Highlands, 44, 45, 106
Highway Historical Marker, 101
Hill, Helen (Mrs. Erle), 24
Hill, Thomas Blount, 64
Hill, Wills, 13
Hillsboro, 13
Hillsborough, 13
Hillsborough Crafts, 84
Hillsborough, Earl of, 13
Hillsborough Garden Club, 33
Hillsborough Historical Society,
   Inc., 37, 38, 55, 72
Hillsborough Military Academy,
   33, 34
Hillsborough Recorder, 33, 35, 36,
   37
Historic American Building, 55
Historic Hillsborough Commis-
   sion, 32, 37, 75
Historical District, 16
Hogg, James, 45, 94, 95
Holden, Thomas, 100
Holden, Governor William, 67
Hollandsworth, D. E., 100
Hollandsworth, Marie (IMrs. D.
   E.), 100
Holmes, Mary, 38
Hooper, Dr. William, 82
Hooper, William (signer of Decla-
   ration of Independence), 37, 79,
   82

Indians, 84, 109
Inn at Teardrop, the (Parks-Rich-
   mond House), 89, 90
Ionic, 86
Iredell, James, 109

Jenkins, Brother Louis, 84
Jenrette, Richard H., 57, 97
Jesus, 62
Johnson, Naile, 102
Johnston, General Joseph E., 34,
   42, 43, 44

Jones, Cadwallader, 59
Jones, Dr. Clarence, Sr., 105
Jones, Clarence, Jr., 105
Jones, James, 105
Jones, Dr. Pride, 73, 74
Jones, Willie, 109
Joscelyn Cheshire, 88

"Kansas," 46
Kennedy, Barbara (Mrs. John P.,
   Jr.), 26, 28, 29
Kennedy, John P., Jr., 26, 28
Kennedy, Sara Beaumont, 88
Kerner, Jule (Korner-Koerner), 31
King George III, 58
"King Street Opera House," 86
King, Thomas, 89
King's Highway, 102
Kirkland, Anne (Mrs. Thomas
   Ruffin), 62

Lindley Nurseries, 105
Lloyd, Alexander ("Alec"), 24, 25
Lloyd, Ida, 24
Lloyd, Sheriff L. B., 71
Lochiel, 104
Lyman, Bishop Theodore, 74

Malett, Peter, 89
Manley, Malthias, 105
"Mansion house," 16
Map (Walking Tour Guide and
   Key), 112–13
Maple Hill, 99, 100
Markers
   Burke, 58
   Churton, 14, 59
   Regulator, 41, 61
Market House, 58
Maryland, 106, 108
Mason, 34
Masonic Hall (Eagle Lodge), 17,
   85, 86
Masterton, Rev. Robert C., 63
Matheson, Elizabeth, 25

McLarty, Dr. Furman, 77
McLarty, Mrs. Furman, 77
McNair, E. D., 44
Messer, Captain, 41
Messer (son of captain), 41
Methodist Church (United), 41
Mickle, Andrew, 44
Mid-Lawn, 69
Milton, 36
Mississippi, Bishop of (William M. Green), 63
Montrose, 47, 48, 49, 96
Moore, Alfred, 15, 50, 51, 104
Moore, Dr. H. W., 75
Moore, Lenna (Mrs. H. W.), 75
Moorefields, 50, 51, 52
Moorefields Foundation, 52
Morris, Robert, 75
Morris Telephone Company, 22, 60
Morse, 35
Morse, Samuel F. B., 35
Mount Bright Baptist Church, 84
Movement, Regulator, 14
Murdock, Henry, 22
Murdock, Mamie (Mrs. William Gordon), 22
Murphey, Archibald D., 82
Murphy, Dr. Michael, 71

Nash, Francis, 79, 92
Nash, Frederick, 82, 93
Nash Law Office ("the Studio"), 92, 93
Nash, Maria, 93
Nash, Sally, 93
Nash-Hooper House, 72, 79–80
Nash-Kollock School, 93
Nashville, Tennessee, 79
Nathaniel Rochester House, 108
National Historic District, 16
National Historic Landmark, 16
National Register of Historic Places, 16
New Bedford, Connecticut, 35, 36

New Bern, 62
New England, 26, 35
New Haven, Connecticut, 35
New York Times, 48
News of Orange County, 48, 49
Nichols, William, 85
Nicks, Emma Woods, 31
Nicks, Rev. Samuel F., 29, 30, 31, 78
Norfolk, Virginia, 70
North Carolina, 67, 82, 86, 103, 106, 107
North Carolina Department of Archives and History, 101
North Carolina General Assembly, 50, 59
North Carolina Medical Society, 67
North Carolina Railroad, 33
North Carolina State Fair, 33
Norwood, James H., 44
Norwood, John C., 105
Norwood, John Wall, 59, 96
Norwood, Robina Hogg, 45, 96
Norwood, William, 45
Norwood-Jones Law Office, 59

Occoneechee Farm (Carr's Farm), 95
Occoneechee Hotel, 45
Old Courthouse (fourth), 55, 57
Old Salem, 58
Old Town Cemetery, 37, 38
Orange County, 13, 14, 84
Orange County Board of Education, 57
Orange County Commissioners, 57
Orange County Courthouse (third), 65
Orange County Courthouse (fifth), 57
Orange County Historical Museum, 57, 84
Orange Hotel, 88

Ordinance of Secession, 33
Over the River, 45, 46, 106
Oxford, 102

Palmer, James, 92
Parker, Africa, 60
Parks, Charles M., 31
Parks, David C., 89
Patterson, David, Sr., 69
Patterson, Mrs. David, Sr., 69
Patterson, James, 92
Patterson-Palmer House, 24, 25, 26, 92
Peace College, 22
Perfec Steriograph, 9, 25
Person, General Thomas, 89
Philadelphia, 106
Phillips, James, 64
Phyfe Room, 28
Piedmont, 21
Pilgrim's Rest (Hasell-Nash House), 75
Poe, Edgar Allan, 29
Poplar Hill, 45, 95
Porter, Ross, 77
Porter, Margaret F. (Mrs. Ross), 77
Presbyterian Church, 28, 75, 82
Preservation Fund, 42–43
Provincial Congress, 15

Quakers, 22, 23, 60, 65
Queen's Gift, 79

Raleigh, 16, 33, 34
Raleigh Standard, 33
Read, 35
Reagan, John H., 42
Redcoats, 47
Regulator Marker, 41, 61
Regulators, 14, 16, 40, 41, 61
Reynolds, Z. Smith Foundation, 43
Rice University, 26
Richmond family, 90
Roberts, Tom, 90

Romanesque, 91
Rosemond, Adelaide (Mrs. Charles G.), 79
Rosemond, Charles G., Sr., 79
Roulhac family, 80
Roulhac-Hamilton House, 80
Rowan County, 16
Ruffin, Anne K. (Mrs. Thomas), 62
Ruffin, Chief Justice Thomas, 57, 62
Ruffin, Jennie L. Hurton (Mrs. Sterling), 74
Ruffin, Peter Browne, 38, 92
Ruffin, Peter Browne house, 38, 92
Ruffin-Roulhac House (Town Hall), 71, 72, 73

St. Mary's Chapel and Churchyard, 100, 101
St. Mary's Friends of the Chapel, 100
St. Mary's Grange, 100
St. Matthew's Churchyard, 62–63
St. Matthew's Episcopal Church, 58, 62
Salisbury, 102
Samuel Gattis House, 86–88
Sandhills, 18
Sanford, Cecil, 80
Sanford, Mary P. (Mrs. Cecil), 80
Sans Souci, 47, 73, 74
Sauthier, Claude Joseph, 17
Sawyer, W. Britton, 88
Scotsmen, 94, 97
Scott, Curtis, 81
Scott, Elsie Carr (Mrs. Curtis), 81
Scott House, 81
Scott, Julius, 81
Semple House, 75
Seven Hearths, 60
Seven Mile Creek, 50
Sharpsburg, 33
Sheffield, Frank, 88

Sheffield, Roxanne (Mrs. Frank), 88
Sherman, General William T., 34, 42, 45
Snipes, Betty J. (Mrs. Jack), 38
Snipes, Jack, 38
South, 36, 106
South Carolina, 106
Southern Living, 48
Spencer's Tavern, 88
Spurgeon, Carrie Waitt (Mrs. J. S.), 33
Spurgeon, Dr. J. S., 31, 32
"Stillhouse branch," 60
"Stillhouse Lott," 60
Strowd, Calvin, 34
Strowd, Octavia, 34
Strudwick, Clement, 26
Strudwick, Edmund, 70
Strudwick, Edmund (artist), 26
Strudwick, Shepperd, Jr., 26, 29
Strudwick, Shepperd, Sr., 26, 28, 29
Strudwick, Susan Read (Mrs. Shepperd, Sr.), 26, 29
Strudwick, Dr. William, 70
"Studio, the" (Nash Law Office), 92, 93
Sunnyside, 47, 48
Sweetbriar College, 26

Tamarind, 26, 27, 28, 29, 71
Tarboro, 44
Taylor, James, 100
Taylor, John, 89
Tew, Colonel Charles, 33, 103
Thompson, Mrs. Bettie, 44
Tidewater, 17
Tory, 61
Town Clock, 57, 58
Town Hall (Ruffin-Roulhac House), 71–73
Transylvania Company, 94
Trumbull, Cdr. Charles, 77
Trumbull, Mrs. Charles, 77

Tryon, Governor William, 17, 40, 41, 79
Tryon's Palace, 62
Tudor, Maggie, 18
Turner, Josiah, 70
Turner-Strudwick House, 70, 71
Twin Chimneys, 88, 89

Uncle Remus, 28
Union, 34, 71
United Methodist Church, 79
University of North Carolina, 22, 50

Veteran's Service Office, 59
Victorian, 69
Virginia, 13, 21, 107

Wake County, 16
War of 1812, 97
Washington, D.C., 42, 48
Washington, George, 16, 106, 107
"Water boy," 103
Webb, Annie Alves Huske, 45
Webb, Annie, 46
Webb House, 67–68
Webb, Dr. James, 45, 67
Webb, James (son of Dr. Webb), 45
Webb, James (grandson of Dr. Webb), 69
Webb, Sarah Frances Cheshire, 46
Webb, Winder, 46
Webster, Noah, 36
Weights and Measures, 84
White, Polly, 100
Whitted, William, Jr., 66
William Whitted House, 66
Williamsburg, 21
Wilmington, 50
Wind in the Forest, The, 79
Winterthur, 28
Witherspoon, John, 82
Witherspoon, Rev. John Knox, 82

Witt, Dr. Mary Ann (Mrs. Ronald), 25
Witt, Dr. Ronald, 25
Woodcarver, 28, 29
World War II, 23

Yanceyville, 106
Yankees, 34

"Yellow House," 22, 23, 60, 92
Yorktown, 15
Younger, Barbara (Mrs. Clifford), 71
Younger, Clifford, 71

Zoning, Historic, 16